A Present From . . .

BY THE SAME AUTHOR

The Naturalist in the Isle of Man
The Industrial Archaeology of the Isle of Man (with Bawden, Qualtrough & Scatchard)

A Present from...

Holiday Souvenirs of the
British Isles

Larch S. Garrad

DAVID & CHARLES
NEWTON ABBOT   LONDON
NORTH POMFRET (VT)   VANCOUVER

For I. O. Evans – who first encouraged me to write

0 7153 7080 4
Library of Congress Catalog Card Number 75–43204
© Larch S. Garrad 1976

Photoset in 11 on 13pt Bembo
and printed in Great Britain
by Redwood Burn Limited, Trowbridge & Esher
for David & Charles (Publishers) Limited
Brunel House Newton Abbot Devon

Published in the United States of America
by David and Charles Inc
North Pomfret Vermont 05053 USA

Published in Canada
by Douglas David & Charles Limited
1875 Welch Street North Vancouver BC.

Contents

Introduction   7

1   Souvenirs: A Historical Perspective   9
Early history – medieval pilgrims' badges – St James's scallop
shells – evolution of the traditional British holiday and mass-
produced souvenirs – development of coastal resorts – home-
produced souvenirs – mass-produced souvenirs – souvenir
trade – modern trends

2   Woodware   24
Arbutus and bog oak manufacturers – Scottish-made souvenir
woodware – early history – transfer-printed or Mauchline
ware – other Scottish souvenir woodware – Tunbridge ware –
foreign woodware – continuing tradition

3   Souvenirs Made from Natural Materials   41
Basketry and rushwork – Irish basketry and rushwork – corkwork, collages, wall plaques, and similar items – horn and
antler souvenirs – seaweed albums and pictures – shells and
shellwork – early history – shellwork – shellwork flowers and
figures – sailors' gifts – shellwork jewellery – embedding in
plastic

4   Geological Souvenirs   59
Early history – Alum Bay and sandwork – Connemara marble
– Derbyshire stone – Cornish and other marbles and serpen-
tines

5   Jewellery   67
Geological jewellery – freshwater pearls – Irish jewellery –
Claddagh ring – jewellery of sentiment – brooches and rings –

charms – metal-plated natural objects – personal ornaments –
Scottish jewellery – luckenbooth brooches

6   Ceramics   84
Armorial china – Goss – other makers of armorial souvenirs –
Belleek – ceramic souvenir makers outside the British Isles –
craft potteries – figures – figure teapots – lithophanes – Parian
and related vitrified biscuit porcelain – ribbon and other wall
plates – Sunderland pink lustre and pink ware – transfer-printed topographical views – origins – later English developments – Doulton – other late developments – wares
personalised or localised only by inscription

7   Metal Souvenirs   109
Brassware – Laxey silver – lead figures – medalets – small
metal boxes

8   . . . But It Is a Souvenir   116
Celluloid, composition, ivorine and other artificial materials –
crested leather goods – glass – painted and engraved items –
glass models – pressed glass – silver glass – local perfumes –
embroidery designs – printed handkerchiefs

Appendices
    1   Major Coastal Resorts   130
    2   Registration Marks   135
    3   Wooden Souvenirs   136
    4   Geological Jewellery   140
    5   Firms Making Armorial China: Provisional List   142
    6   Ceramic Souvenir Types   144

Bibliography   152
Acknowledgements   155
Index   156

Introduction

Souvenir: Thing given, kept etc to recall the past, memento (of . . . place, etc) – *Concise Oxford Dictionary*.

An essential part of the traditional holiday is the carrying home of some trifle to be given a place of honour as a reminder of the annual visit to the seaside, or a day trip to some pleasure resort. There can be few households which do not cherish at least one such souvenir. When it has been inherited from an older generation it may have considerable charm as an example of vernacular art, and its owners will want to know more about it. British keepsakes vary from Aunt Emily's thimble, in a beautifully fashioned sycamore box printed with a view of Douglas Bay by Smith's of Mauchline, to Uncle Albert's bright peppermint-rock-pink moustache cup, heavily embellished with edelweiss and proclaiming in florid gold script that it is 'A present from Margate' but, on its base, that it was made in Germany. Most such souvenirs were mass-produced but, as the rising prices asked in antique shops indicate, they are well worth collecting. The Victorian interest in antiquities and the widespread use of native raw materials that was fostered by the Great Exhibition of 1851 produced much that is attractive, particularly Irish and Scottish jewellery, which often used Celtic designs. This is just as much a souvenir as the most pedestrian topographical ware.

Unfortunately, there has been a tendency to sneer at souvenirs merely because they are 'popular'. It is hoped that this introduction will help to change this, for souvenirs interest many, whether or not they have pretensions to being art historians. The antecedents of the items offered as 'A Present From . . .' are discovered, so far as local records, much depleted by two world wars, allow and modern developments are outlined.

In general, treatment within the chapters is alphabetical, not chronological, one notable exception being that jewellery using semi-precious stones has been brought to the beginning, along with other geological souvenirs.

No single volume could cover the whole field comprehensively. Here we concentrate on items associated with particular places; articles designed to recall events or people are omitted save where, as with Shakespeariana and Burnsiana, they are essentially souvenirs of a place.

LSG

1 Souvenirs: A Historical Perspective

Modern usage allows a souvenir to be both something given as a reminder of the donor and something kept by the original purchaser or collector. The collecting of reminders of travels, and the taking back of presents to show that the traveller has remembered those at home, are as old as human history. Obviously, only the most durable survive in archaeological contexts and their significance may be conjectural, but we know that Minoan pots, painted with beautiful designs of nautilus shells, fish and other marine life have been found far up the Nile in Egypt. Perhaps, like the pots with distinctive Pratt lids used for Margate shrimp paste, they once housed some special delicacy. The ancient trade in shells will be described later. Travellers in classical Greece also purchased fine pots. Sometimes the quality alone is sufficient to mark them out but they may also be localised by symbols, like Athene's owl, which proclaim their origin as clearly as the traditional words 'A present from . . .'

Many of these ancient souvenirs seem to have had a religious (or magical or superstitious) significance. Thus visitors to classical shrines would purchase statuettes of the deity honoured there, or associated emblems. Like votive candles of modern times, these might be offered at the shrine itself but they might also be carried home. Rather later, pilgrims to Christian shrines, particularly those of the Holy Land, proved a ready market for religious tokens, ranging from a palm leaf to enough pieces of the 'true cross' and 'authentic nails' to build several good-sized boats or bone fragments, frequently not even human, of assorted saints, and ribbon-like scraps of fabric which had merely touched more authentic corporal remains. They also included relics of the past endowed with alleged magical powers. Fragments of Egyptian mummies were used medicinally, both 'to be taken' and in curious rites. A figure of the Egyptian god Osiris was recovered from a grave at Rushen Abbey in the Isle of Man. Presumably, someone had convinced a traveller that this was a symbol of the resurrection, but of what arduous journey was it a souvenir? Similarly, the excavators of the monastic site on Burry Holmes in Wales identified a scrap of stone from well-known quarries in Sparta. This stone seems to have had some mystical significance at a very early date; it has also been identified from the palace of Minos at Knossos in Crete in a Bronze Age context, but how and why did it reach Wales?

MEDIEVAL PILGRIMS' BADGES

In the medieval period, a pilgrimage might offer common people their only opportunity to travel. The main period of popularity of pilgrimages, such as provided the connecting link for Chaucer's *Canterbury Tales*, was the thirteenth to fifteenth centuries. A considerable supporting industry of inns and shops selling specialities to the travellers grew up along the most used routes, such as that leading to the shrine of St Thomas at Canterbury, the Pilgrims' Way. At the shrines themselves, revenue was obtained by selling various tokens which could be taken home as evidence of travel. A contemporary of Chaucer, Erasmus, describes in his *Perigrinatio Religionis Erga* a pilgrim who had been to the shrines of St James at Compostella in Spain and Our Lady of Boulogne. He wears the scallop shells traditionally associated with the former, bead bracelets, straw chains and 'images of tin and lead'. These last are among the earlier souvenirs to survive. They normally take the form of an emblem associated with the dedication of the shrine and were cast in stone or metal moulds. The right to produce them was jealously guarded.

Not all the medals were kept as souvenirs. A very high proportion

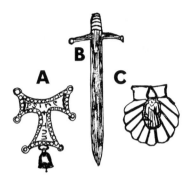

Medieval pilgrims' badges found in the Thames at London: (A) Tau cross of St Antoine de Viennois, France; (B) Sword, the emblem of St Paul, from St Paul's Cathedral, London; (C) Scallop shell with figure of the saint, from the shrine of St James of Compostella, Galicia, Spain.

of those known have been recovered from river crossings, particularly of the Thames and Seine. Those from the Thames have been explained as having been associated with the shrine of St Thomas on London Bridge, from which the pilgrims might start. It is possible that they were cast into the river by the returned pilgrims as a symbol of the ending of their journey and of any penances they might have undertaken for its duration. However, it is more probable that they were thrown into the river as a superstitious survival of early sacrifices to deities of crossings, and this custom should be associated with that by which modern visitors throw coins into water 'for luck,' or to ensure a return visit. Sometimes this habit is deliberately exploited for charity but it seems to be totally irrational. Why should part of the modern waterworks at Cheddar Gorge be saluted in this way?

ST JAMES'S SCALLOP SHELLS

In addition to the metal badges showing a scallop shell, which have been recovered as far away as Copenhagen, pilgrims to the shrine of St James at Compostella were offered real scallop shells. The metal badges were usually worn in the hat and the shells sold at the shrine were also attached to garments. Selling them was so lucrative that excommunication was sometimes resorted to in order to stop illicit trading, which presumably did not pay due tithe. The journey to Compostella was so popular that the scallop shell became virtually synonymous with pilgrimage. The symbol was associated also with the shrine at Mont St Michel in France. Unfortunately, no example of a scallop shell which is certainly a pilgrim's souvenir and not a relic of the dinner table has ever been found. Some of the useful and beautiful Mediterranean pottery excavated on medieval sites in England may also have been brought home by returning pilgrims. Most of the other souvenirs of pilgrimage have proved less durable. Were Erasmus's pilgrim's straw chains plaited like Victorian hair watchguards? Were they emblems of the vanities of this world or, like those offered at St Audrey's fair – from which is derived that epithet so suited to many souvenirs, *tawdry* – merely attractive but cheap? Were the bead bracelets charms, rosaries or ornaments? Contemporary literature offers little help. However, it is clear that much of the early history of souvenirs is bound up with religious observances. Even after the reformation the fairs once associated with saints' days survived. Many of the earlier types of souvenirs, particularly in china, evolved from the cheap, bright 'fairings' sold to the cheerful crowd at such gatherings.

TRADITIONAL
AND MASS-PRODUCED SOUVENIRS

The Industrial Revolution created the traditional British holiday since this was essentially an annual exodus by town dwellers who, before the time of mass car ownership, would otherwise scarcely see a natural landscape. Industrialisation concentrated large numbers of people together in surroundings in which a holiday at home was frequently no pleasure. It also ensured that more and more people had both the transport and the financial means to make a holiday, ultimately their legal entitlement, worthwhile. If the lists of visitors and their home

Plate 1 A selection of typical souvenirs.

towns which appear in local newspapers are an adequate guide, the
northern resorts' initial rise was in response to the needs of the wives
and families of the newly-rich factory owners and the higher grades
of supervisory staff. As is still customary in some continental countries, the families would enjoy a prolonged break while their working
menfolk joined them for shorter periods. Few northern resorts
remained 'select' for long. The spinning and weaving districts early
established the custom of wakes weeks, in which a whole town
ceased work simultaneously. Once the railway system had grown,
wakes weeks created the perfect market for mass travel. Whole
streets would empty into a special train and spend their holiday in the

same group of boarding houses. (Is this the explanation of the curious Douglas custom by which the guests in the seafront boarding houses sit on seats on the front steps and *talk* while waiting for their evening meal?)

By contrast, many of the southern resorts mainly catered for a more middle-class market. Londoners had always enjoyed trips to Margate or Southend but, for example, Frinton, Worthing and Bournemouth remained obstinately 'superior' well into the twentieth century. The pattern of wives, children and nannies summering at the seaside became well established but there was seldom the really large scale collective move to the same resort. Despite heroic efforts by publicity officers, the traditional catchment areas of coastal resorts established in the nineteenth century persist. Londoners do not favour Blackpool or the Isle of Man and the textile towns send few visitors to the south-east. However, twentieth-century mobility based on personal transport and motorways may break down this tradition. In 2070 it may be worthwhile to look for 1970 presents from Douglas in London and presents from Brighton in Bolton, but today the place to look for a resort's souvenirs is its main source of visitors.

Development of coastal resorts

Coastal resorts began to gain in popularity, partly at the expense of the old inland spas, before the beginning of the nineteenth century, and the ascendancy of the seaside was fully established by 1850. As an illustration of this trend, Mavor's *The British Tourist* published in 1798 describes many of the beauty spots still patronised by modern (motor) coach tourists (the Dovey valley, Strata Florida, Tintern and Beaulieu abbeys, the New Forest and, in Ireland, Blarney, Glendalough and Killarney) but of the thirty-three main seaside towns individually listed in *Adam's Illustrated Descriptive Guide to the Watering Places* fifty years later only seven, mainly in Wales, are even mentioned. The rapid expansion of the railway system did much to foster this growth of coastal holidays. Brighton, once the haunt of the fashionable, became a home for commuters while Margate and Ramsgate, 'fallen time out of mind, under the ban of cockneydom' brought in by the hoys, large single-decked boats, became even more crowded. For a time, Southend, lacking a direct rail link with London, was considered more select. Some towns welcomed the railway while others fought against the vulgarity that followed in its wake. Weston-super-Mare decided that it should not reach right into the still-growing town and lived to regret its isolation on an inconvenient loop line. One of the immediate uses to which new lines were put was the day excursion and it was the mass travel for pleasure that arose from railway mania that produced the market for mass-produced cheap souvenirs.

When deciding whether early souvenirs of a particular resort are likely to be common or rare it is as well to discover something of its early history. The date when the nearest railway stations were connected to large population centres may be important. However, it should be remembered that water transport, particularly from Liverpool and London, remained viable for a long time. Thus when the railway reached Liverpool both the Isle of Man and the North Wales resorts were within easy reach of the industrial Midlands and north. Once a resort was established it often grew very rapidly, the 'small but thriving watering place' of Blackpool, for example. Some helped themselves with judicious changes of name. Walton le Soken became Walton-on-the-Naze and one of the several Westons of north Somerset became 'super-mare'.

Home-produced Souvenirs

In the more remote and underpopulated areas little except ingenuity was available to local people to provide souvenirs for their visitors. Natural raw materials might be offered unworked. For example, Sir George Head, in his *Home Tour* published by John Murray in 1841, describes the genesis of the trade in the distinctive apple-green stone commonly known as *Iona marble*. When he visited Iona he saw 'a group of children, chiefly little girls, each with a plate in her hand containing pebbles and shells for sale . . . among these specimens the light green stone especially peculiar to the island, was in tolerable abundance'. Fossils and fine mineral specimens were also sold. In mining areas the sale of the latter was often an important source of income for widows, and crippled or retired miners who frequently, as at Laxey, outlived the mine. Like other nineteenth century fashions, the geological souvenir is also being revived.

Local delicacies and foodstuffs which, like Cheddar cheese, fish pastes or ketchups, Manx kippers and Yarmouth bloaters would travel fairly well, would also be offered. With the establishment of an efficient parcel post service these often became a major source of income, and less durable goods such as Cornish and Devonshire cream were added to the 'You write the address, we do the rest' trade. In most cases all traces of such edible souvenirs have completely vanished, although the quality of the boxes in which Manx kippers were posted is such that some late nineteenth century examples have survived to bring joy to collectors of printed ephemera. At a time before takeovers and national advertising almost ensured that the goods stocked by grocers in holiday resorts were identical with those in the holidaymakers' home towns, local products, particularly when they were peculiar to the area, might have been taken home as presents. Thus it may be suggested that, to some extent, even the famous printed pot lids used by Margate firms on their shrimp pastes could be considered as souvenirs, although their primary purpose was advertisement.

Mass-produced souvenirs

Once a mass market evolved, inexpensive trifles produced in factories rather than workshops became the commoner type of souvenir. The southern resorts, Brighton, Worthing, Margate, etc, had their first pieces localised by *A trifle from* . . . and *A present from* . . . before the beginning of the period under consideration. Little boxes, whether Bilston enamel or Tunbridge ware – see the illustration on p. 37 – were particularly popular. Many potteries, such as those of Bristol and Lowestoft, similarly localised their ordinary wares.

The next step was the addition of a topographical view. Topographical view china started with engravings applied by a technique evolved by Sadler and Green. The engravings became the common stock-in-trade of souvenir manufacturers. Virtually identical subjects appear on vast range of novelty printed ephemera such as fans, cards, boxes and baskets, in guide books, on Scottish woodware, ceramics and textiles. In time, the engraved block gave way to the photographic plate.

The other main means of localising a mass-produced souvenir is the addition of some local emblem to the basic shape. This may be as simple as the shamrock of Ireland, the tailless cat or three-legs of the Isle of Man, the head of Shakespeare for Stratford-on-Avon, or the Lincoln imp. However, many resorts became boroughs and were granted arms, and a few already had heraldic devices. Thus heraldic, or armorial, or crested, souvenirs were born. Goss claimed to produce a souvenir for every place with a coat of arms, and there were a host of imitators. Not all the flatterers were as scrupulous in their heraldry, and curious devices appear to symbolise uninhabited spots. Lighthouses, sea creatures and local folk heroes are prominent. In the twentieth century, makers of crested souvenirs often reduce the number of dies required by using county arms combined with varying placenames. 'Crests' had spread from ceramics to metal and leather by the beginning of the twentieth century.

The antecedents of the trivial joke souvenir, inherently ephemeral, are impossible to chronicle. Many seem to epitomise the music hall joke, but he who first gave three-dimensional form to the bad puns, landlady and lavatory jokes will remain (deservedly?) unknown. As far as human memory can determine, most of them seem to be very durable. Female legs and bosoms, trick glasses, etc go on from year to year. The author has heard of a 'Present from Blackpool' fake glass of beer which had been trawled up off Iceland, complete with barnacles encrusted on the head.

The souvenir trade

At the beginning of the nineteenth century, specialist souvenir shops were uncommon apart from those in the long-established spa towns. As the demand grew for some trifle as a gift or reminder of a pleasant holiday, shops selling guide books or fancy goods would add localised items to their stock. The number of specialised shops probably increased with the growth of a resort and in some areas advertising in guide books and the press indicates considerable competition.

Plate 2 Souvenirs for the needlewoman: (1) and (2) Penelope embroidery packs, (3) Late Mauchline box with photographic view, (4) Ivory needle case with peepshow views of Brighton, (5) Early Mauchline thimble case. Bog oak souvenirs: (6) Brooch, (7) Tinker's pot, (8) Inkwell, and (9) Pincushion in shape of traditional Irish pots.

In Isle of Man guide books, view albums and similar printed items are advertised in the press for some fifteen years before any other type of souvenir is offered, perhaps because they were produced by the printers. After 1849, a few firms advertised regularly in the Manx papers. Goods described include, in approximate order of appearance, workboxes with the Manx arms and motto, local scents, pebble jewellery, jewellery with local emblems, exotic shells, fancy baskets, items decorated with seaweed, Irish spar jewellery and Scottish topographical woodware. One unchanged souvenir, Mona Bouquet scent (created by Okell in 1852 and taken over by Greensill in 1861), is still available, but the palm for durability in the souvenir trade must surely go to Iona marble and Derbyshire spar jewellery and ornaments, both of which were sold before 1800.

It is difficult to discover how often souvenirs were advertised in the early nineteenth century. Very few local shops, as opposed to services, had notices in Manx papers before the 1840s so the advertising of souvenirs may merely reflect the general growth of advertising practice. Research by Dr Eric Glasgow suggests that Southport firms commonly did not advertise in the local press. This may indicate a greater sale of Manx *national* as opposed to English *local* papers to visitors in the period before a daily paper was an automatic purchase. In Man there is an unexplained reduction in newspaper advertisements in the approximate period 1908–14.

Data on the amount spent by individuals on souvenirs is hard to obtain and changes in the value of money and the level of wages make meaningful comparisons difficult. At the end of the nineteenth century, sixpence to a shilling seems to be the usual price range. This would cover such diverse items as small gold and silver brooches, cotton handkerchiefs, some china and wooden items – all with topographical views – and the smallest size in local scent. It was also the price range of illustrated guides and view albums. Penny books and penny souvenirs, or even a number of identical items for a penny, catered for the less well off and those needing several individual gifts. The relation of expenditure on souvenirs to other costs, such as transport to the resort and accommodation, obviously varied but in the Isle of Man seems to have been approximately 10–20 per cent of the price of the journey and 5–10 per cent of a day's lodging, or little more than the price of a single meal. A visiting family would normally buy a number of gifts for friends and relations, as well as at least one piece for their own home. The author has repeatedly been told 'so-and-so brought me something back every year', or 'my auntie always bought presents for all her nieces'. Honeymoon couples would often buy each other gifts for their new home. When times were hard the gifts might be no more than 'six sticks of rock, a penny' but numerous collections testify to the frequent purchase of more durable souvenirs.

It appears unlikely that there has been any major change in souvenir buying although the school group with a majority of children with money to spend on gifts seem to be a post-1945 phenomenon. Research by Brian Deane of the Irish Tourist Board highlights differences in spending patterns between North American and British visitors to Ireland. The 61·2 per cent of visitors from the United Kingdom spent fractionally less than the mere 13·2 per cent originating from North America. This will reflect other factors besides greater spending potential – 61·1 per cent of the UK visitors purchasing souvenirs in Ireland had incomes under £3,000 as against 7 per cent of those from North America. The longer and more expensive the journey to the resort the less often it will be repeated. Thus the long-distance tourist may be willing to buy more expensive goods. Furthermore, many Irish products are freely available at comparable prices elsewhere in the British Isles. At least a fifth of purchases by value consist of tweeds and woollen clothing, while the more trivial souvenirs account for only some 7 per cent. Over half the British visitors bought products costing less than £5 and virtually another quarter paid between £5 and £10. Just under 9 per cent of British visitors bought no souvenirs at all in Ireland. This is probably a fairly typical modern pattern of spending by the British on holiday. While the costs of travel have probably risen proportionately more than those of traditional boarding house accommodation, it would suggest that the

Plates 3-4 Display and selling of craft souvenirs as an integral part of a tourist attraction: a craft shop in Dublin (*top*) and the sales and display area at Castle Wynd Studios, Aviemore, Scotland (*below*).

nineteenth century relationship between total holiday costs and souvenir purchases has remained constant.

MODERN TRENDS

Space in this book has been given to modern trends partly because the souvenir market is still growing and if developments are not documented now their history will be shrouded in the same mystery as those preceding. Moreover, a souvenir is basically undateable since those of the earlier period reappear on the market with considerable frequency. According to figures quoted by Anthony Smith in *Beside the Seaside,* 30 million holidaymakers annually visit British resorts. (In the popularity polls, Blackpool is the easy winner with $8\frac{1}{2}$ million while Brighton sees $4\frac{1}{2}$ million and Cornwall $2\frac{1}{2}$ million.) He observed that when the last make their obligatory stop at Land's End, the view, 'toilets, tea and treasured purchases' occupy them for less than an hour before they leave. If the Irish figures, which suggest that about 90 per cent of British visitors purchase at least one item, hold good for the British Isles as a whole then the number of souvenirs in circulation must be staggering.

Apart from the trends outlined in later chapters, one contemporary development remains to be mentioned. This is the attempt by official bodies such as the Irish Tourist Board, the Highlands and Islands Development Board and the Council for Small Industries in Rural Areas (CoSIRA) to foster the production of craftwork. Their aim is both to improve the aesthetic quality (and thus the attractiveness?) of souvenirs and to promote viable industries in areas which may otherwise lack markets for their products. Their success must be obvious to all but it is a depressing fact of the modern souvenir trade that there is a tendency to uniformity not only between areas of the United Kingdom but within the whole area exploited by the travel industry. Bullfighting posters, olive wood and carved animals are as common in Southend as in Spain, Israel or East Africa. The craft souvenirs of Greece are sold beside Portsoy marble, and Siamese silverware competes with the work of Welsh craftsmen. So far, moon rock undoubt-edly holds the record as the dearest ever souvenir, but how long before 'A present from the moon' joins those from Blackpool and Berlin, or a stick of rock lettered thus is produced by the factory which already supplies Mecca?

2 Woodware

Wooden souvenirs have been the speciality of the eponymous Spa (now in Belgium) for a considerable period and were produced also in Tunbridge Wells, an important watering place from the end of the seventeenth century. At the beginning of the nineteenth century, those who could afford to take holidays of any length could commission the work of craftsmen and pay them quite considerable sums. There must have been many other local woodcarvers who, like Stivens of Laurencekirk, took advantage of the passage of the coaches to sell more luxury items than the local people required, but the Scottish snuff box trade became the basis for what was to be perhaps the largest and most far-reaching trade in wooden souvenirs, the transfer-printed or Mauchline ware with topographical views. The names of the other opportunists have largely been lost.

Even after the rise of the mass produced souvenir, local workers continued to take advantage of the passing visitor, sometimes even to the extent of profiteering, as in the market for lucky charms. Just as glass workers sometimes made small items in their own time to sell to supplement their wages, joiners and other woodworkers might make a few pieces. For example, the author's collection includes a veneered workbox with an inner tray and padded silk lining which was acquired in a junk shop for a very small sum. It is an unmarked and unremarkable example of a typical middle class Victorian possession. However, she has also seen another, virtually identical apart from the colour of the lining, which was in the possession of the original owner's granddaughter. Thus it is possible to deduce that these were a sideline of a Stratford-on-Avon undertaker, joiner and upholsterer, made with the surplus from larger scale work, and sold in that tourist-haunted town. Later in the nineteenth century, working people were offered excursions from which they usually wanted to bring home souvenirs. Innumerable small boxes marked 'A present from . . . ' helped to sate this growing demand for tokens for stay-at-home friends and of remembrances of happy hours. Some must have been the work of local firms and some mass produced in Britain. As the demand for cheap items grew, a large percentage were made abroad. The history of the more important manufactures is given here.

ARBUTUS AND BOG OAK ORNAMENT MANUFACTURERS

As the railways opened up Ireland to greater numbers of tourists a wide range of native raw materials was used to produce essentially Irish souvenirs for them. From the late 1840s, shops in Killarney offered small wooden ornaments '. . . similar to the Tunbridgeware goods: they are formed from the wood of the beautiful arbutus tree . . . it is capable of receiving the finest polish, together with the hoofs of the wild deer, is made into snuff boxes, rings, and a variety of fancy articles'. In 1857, Jeremiah O'Connor advertised in Slater's *Directory* 'Lakes of Killarney Interesting to visitors Arbutus Bog Oak and Wild Deer's Hoof Factory . . . Next Door to Kenmare Arms Hotel, nearly opposite the Church . . . Tables Davenports Draft Boards Work Boxes &c'. According to the same directory there were two more rival factories, owned by Jeremiah Crimmin and James Egan, where visitors could watch the craftsmen at work and commission special items, and a fourth shop, kept by Edward Eagar. The existence of the latter suggests that there was something of a cottage industry in the area but only Daniel Connell of Dublin showed arbutus wood 'card cases &c' at the Great Exhibition. The arbutus, popularly known as the strawberry tree (botanically *Arbutus unedo*), is abundant in Killarney and forms part of the unique Lusitanian flora of south-

Plate 5 Irish arts and crafts: the display, set against a traditional open hearth, includes printed and woven textiles, pottery, ironwork, turned and sculpted wood, rushwork baskets, and a bowl and egg in Connemara marble.

west Ireland.

Bog oak, the timber found in peat bags, also lent itself to the production of ornamental pieces. In 1857, there were eight 'bog oak ornament manufacturers' in Dublin, including Cornelius and Jeremiah Goggin, at 13 Nassau Street and 74 Grafton Street respectively. In 1892, the latter firm was still offering 'Table ornaments carved out of Irish Bog Oak; Jewel Caskets, Writing Suites, Cigar Cabinets, Candelabras, Crosses, Brooches, Necklets, Earrings, Scarf Pins, Celtic

Gold and Silver, Connemara Marble and Irish Spar Jewellery, Bog Oak Sticks &c'. E.M. Goggin & Co of 20 Nassau Street also had 'Irish Bog Oak Carvings and Jewellery, Candlesticks, Sticks in carved wood, Blackthorns mounted and unmounted . . .'

Bog-oak trifles: crudely carved earrings and brooch sold in the Isle of Man but probably made in Ireland.

From the advertisements it is clear that quite sizeable furniture was made, but the more portable items were doubtless more abundant and popular. Writing cases, desk sets, workboxes and similar fairly useful pieces are quite common. They are usually fairly plain, although contrasting inlay of arbutus, holly, metal, 'Irish diamonds' or mother of pearl, occurs. The shapes and fittings are frequently similar to examples not produced for the souvenir market, but novelties abound. For example, the author's collection includes a charming inkwell in the shape of the three-legged iron pot used for cooking over an open turf fire. The body, lid and tapered legs are turned from bog oak, the two side handles are shaped from wire and there is a clear glass liner. She has also seen a pin cushion and a thimble case in the same shape. Copies of standing crosses are common. A great many of the medium sized bog oak ornaments were turned. Chip carving may sometimes indicate the product of an individual worker, and not that of a small factory equipped with a lathe and woodworking tools.

Bog oak jewellery follows contemporary fashions in its shapes. It is often floral but harps, shamrocks, Killarney ferns and similar 'typically Irish' motifs also proclaim its origin. Bog oak might be combined with mounts in silver, or less precious metals, and seed or freshwater pearls. It was popular as mourning jewellery, thus sharing the Victorian vogue for Whitby jet. The firms which made bog oak personal ornaments were usually working jewellers who used other materials also: Waterhouse & Co of 25 Dame Street, Dublin, 'the Queen's Jewellers', for example. (See Chapter 5).

A stick was an essential adjunct to a gentleman's dress in the nineteenth century and sticks of a dark colour were popular with older women also. Blackthorn sticks would be thought suitable for rural travelling and the more elegant turned, carved and mounted examples would be acceptable gifts. The comic shillelagh belongs more to the era of the tripper, but Victorians and Edwardians thought a knobbly and substantial blackthorn appropriate to rustic life. Riding crops and parasol handles were also made. Such is the quantity of bog oak souvenirs that it is clear that not all the peat diggings of Ireland would have produced sufficient timber to make them. Many pieces must have started life in the forests of Scandinavia or North America rather than in the geological past of Ireland, but while recipes for artificially darkening wood certainly exist much of the finer work is undoubtedly genuine bog oak.

SCOTTISH-MADE SOUVENIR WOODWARE

Early history

The earlier Scottish woodware souvenirs were almost exclusively snuffboxes and were initially sold mainly in the district where they were made. The trade increased after a selftaught craftsman, the crippled James Sandy of Alyth in Perthshire, evolved a method of cutting an integral hinge mechanically. The integral hinge ensured that a rectangular box would remain sufficiently airtight to keep snuff in good condition. After its general introduction, boxes made by professionals were usually this shape. The invention seems to have been taken over by Charles Stiven who set up shop in the stagecoach office at Laurencekirk, Kincardineshire, about 1783 under the patronage of Lord Gardenstone, Superior of that town. Spa in Belgium had long been noted for its decorated woodware. Lord Gardenstone gave further impetus to the development of the Scottish industry when, in 1787, he induced Mr Brixhe from Spa to go to Laurencekirk and give instruction in methods of painting decoration on woodware. The Belgian painter settled in Scotland for some time but there were never a large number of workshops in Kincardineshire.

Charles Stiven was joined in his business by his son Alexander, and it seems that as early as 1819 boxes made by them might be marked 'and son', although in 1837 Pigot & Co's *Directory* still lists the firm as 'Charles Stiven, original inventor and tea caddies, card and ladies workboxes &c'. under the heading of snuffbox makers. This directory also mentions Robert M'Donald, who was Stiven's son-in-law. At various dates at least two of Stiven's ex-apprentices, W. Crab and William (of W. & G.) Milner, also appear to have worked independently. As indicated by the notice above, the Laurencekirk firms attempted to counteract the decline in trade when the taking of snuff became unfashionable by expanding their range, but the eastern Scottish woodware industry faded away by about 1870. The early boxes, when ornamented at all, were hand-painted. Later, the Stivens seem to have made a speciality of using wood with historical or literary associations which were inscribed on the box. Identifiable boxes by Kincardineshire makers are rather uncommon and even the Stivens' workshop, royal warrant holders though they became, cannot have been large. They, and their immediate competitors, catered to a localised luxury trade. It seems possible that only the better quality goods were marked.

The integral hinge, as produced in Laurencekirk, was also called the secret hinge as the ends of the metal pin, which linked the interlocking knuckles on the lid and the box, were concealed by wooden plugs. There was a carefully fostered story to the effect that '. . . the very nice manner in which the hinges are constructed is admirable, and although in this part of the box, many imitations have been attempted, all have failed to rival the original manufacturer'. This information is part of the entry, in the same 1837 directory as that quoted earlier, concerning Cumnock and Auchinleck in Ayrshire, which

> . . . is celebrated for the manufacture of those beautiful wooden snuff boxes, a species of trade which originated here nearly thirty years since, and, with some few exceptions as Laurencekirk, Catrine and Mauchline, is still confined to Cumnock . . . Plane tree is the wood used in the manufacture, and great ingenuity is evinced in adorning the lids with devices, which is chiefly performed by boys . . .

Since there are fifteen makers and five painters listed below this statement, and a further four makers noted in Catrine and Mauchline, the compiler of this directory presumably did not share the illusion, fostered by some later writers, that the trade was wholly new in the area. In fact it seems to have started very soon after that in Kincardineshire but the manufacture of souvenir woodware did not decline to the same extent with the fall in the demand for snuffboxes.

While snufftaking was still fashionable, the rate of growth of the industry was considerable for a luxury trade producing hand-painted, often commissioned, and expensive goods. William Crawford of Cumnock seems to have been the only snuffbox maker in 1811 but when the 1825 *Commercial Dictionary of Scotland* was produced the 'original maker' (not inventor as Stiven at Laurencekirk claimed to be) had five rivals and there were two painters in addition who presumably decorated plain boxes made by the others. Twelve years later Crawford, three Crichtons (Adam, David '& Co' and Peter) and Alexander Lammie were still trading as box makers.

In all about fifty firms, mainly in Auchinleck, Catrine, Cumnock and Mauchline, existed in the first half of the nineteenth century. Towards the end of the period the more elaborate designs were joined by simple chequered patterns and tartans. Marked pieces, if only because of the larger number of producers involved, are less uncommon than from the Laurencekirk factories but are by no means plentiful. Cigar smoking gradually replaced snufftaking among the fashionable and although the more enterprising firms diversified, such as William & Andrew Smith, snuffbox makers '(& cigar cases &c to His Majesty)', most of the smaller family workshops closed well before they could display their wares at the Great Exhibition, although some survivors must have supplied the London firms which exhibited Scottish woodware.

Transfer-printed or Mauchline ware

By a series of fortunate chances it has proved possible for Lord David Stewart and E.H. and E.R. Pinto to document the history of the Smith's of Mauchline, who seem to have initiated the production of transfer-printed woodware. This was to become one of the most abundant, popular and widespread forms of wooden souvenir and to be commonly known, because of the location of their factory, as Mauchline ware. The firm, as W. & A. Smith, is known to have been trading by 1823. Their earliest specialities were sycamore (confusingly known in Scotland as plane) snuffboxes, decorated in pen-and-ink, and wooden-backed strops for the then ubiquitous cut-throat razors. The possession of a royal warrant was advertised by transfer-printing the arms of the king, William IV, on the strops. The ease of this method of decoration and the pleasing effect it produced on the even, pale colour of the sycamore was not lost on the Smiths.

The design was in fact transferred by a method very similar to that perfected by Sadler & Green of Liverpool for decorating ceramics. The design was printed from an engraved plate on to special Japanese paper. The print was then varnished on its face, placed face down on the recently shellac-ed surface of the article to be decorated, and left to dry. After drying, which took up to two hours depending on humidity, the paper was removed with the aid of a damp cloth, leaving the ink impression behind. More and more tourists were following their Queen to Scotland and transfer-printing was clearly an ideal means of converting a mass produced article into the souvenir of a particular locality. Gradually the firm became almost self sufficient, making its own boxes and their decoration with the aid of sophisticated machinery which they patented.

Views appeared on a vast range of sycamore objects, of varying utility, to house every conceivable adjunct to the toilet table or writing desk. Sewing aids also, such as cases for bodkins, crochet hooks, knitting needles (and guards to prevent stitches being dropped when the work was stored), needles, pins and thimbles, an incredible variety of novelty tape measures, silk winders, tatting shuttles, thread

Plate 6   Mauchline ware: early transfer-printed pieces.

barrels and waxers and holders for balls of wool, together with work boxes in which to store them, accounted for a substantial part of the range. On the whole, the items were fairly small, sufficient to display a single view to advantage.

Their success in catering for the insatiable demands of tourists was such that the firm opened a warehouse in Birmingham, nearer the established heart of the 'toy' trade, in 1829. The original partnership split up in 1843 and the two brothers then traded separately. After the death of William, in 1846, the surviving brother revived the firm's old name with his son, another William, as partner. Premises in Birmingham were retained until 1904 and production continued, albeit on a diminished scale, until a disastrous fire in the Scottish box works in 1933. Finally, the founder's grandson, yet another William, retired early in 1937 and Smith's of Mauchline ceased to exist.

At the height of its expansion the firm had something of a monopoly of transfer-printed woodware and produced souvenirs for most of the resorts in the British Isles as well as Australia, the USA and the continental watering places most frequented by the British. Proof of the extent of their market has survived in the form of the original printing plates, acquired by the Pintos, and a traveller's album. Such a profitable trade could not last unshared, and foreign as well as local firms attempted to compete. The precise origin of the rival products is often cloaked by 'Manufactured abroad', an ironical counterpart to 'Importé' on Smith's French views, which had been made at a time when their activity extended even to producing advertising souvenirs for French drapers and the makers of Singer sewing machines. German and even the still-imitative Japanese producers made similar wares and, regrettably, few items are marked. Not surprisingly, part of this vast quantity of goods has survived and few sellers of less-important antiques and bygones can fail to produce a box or two. The views known to have been used by Smith's are listed in *Tunbridge and Scottish Souvenir Woodware* but other examples, if in good condition, are hardly less attractive.

It seems that at no time were Smith's products limited to transfer-printed ware. They started producing hand-painted tartan boxes quite early and later simplified the manufacture by applying printed sheets to wooden bases. The name of the clan was usually given on the boxes. Tartan ware was apparently popular in France since items were made exclusively for the French market. The range in tartan was somewhat different from the transfer-printed souvenirs and included ingredients for the all-tartan interior which has sometimes been held up as the epitome of Victorian taste. It is often forgotten that once the prohibition of tartan (imposed with the intention of destroying clan unity after the Stuarts' unsuccessful attempt to win back the throne) had fallen into abeyance it had again become the appropriate adornment of the state of the clan chief. Even the Lords of Mann owned a set of Scotch plaid bed-curtains, complemented by wall hangings in red, white, yellow and purple flannel, according to an inventory of about 1693. It is to be hoped that the light was poor or the colours were less strident than their description would suggest.

Later tartan ware is less elegant and there is a tendency to combine the attractions of a genuine Scottish tartan with a view, not always of a Scottish scene. Smith's stopped making tartanware about the end of the nineteenth century but the eclipse in its popularity, if such there was, was only temporary and other firms subsequently more than filled the gap. It is probable that needlebooks and similar items, with enamelled views on domed plaques surrounded by a tartan ground, were German made. Certainly some of their scenes closely resemble those on the German glass paperweights. Smith's themselves made tartan items with views, some of which were machine-coloured by a process they patented.

In an attempt to compete with the cheaper and more highly-mechanised imports, various novel finishes for wooden souvenirs were evolved. Among the earliest were Scoto-Damascene and Scoto-Russian work which was shown at the Great Exhibition. Both involved covering the base with metal foil, but little survives since even Smith's superb glue could not retain the foil. The former was machine-decorated with the aid of William Smith's patent ruling machine while the latter had a design engraved through a paint finish to produce an effect akin to true niello, with metal threads showing against a dark ground. Some of the transfer-printed ware had painted floral sprays, and boxes with painted decoration seem to have been made alongside the more mechanised products. One wonders if some of this work was made by smaller workshops and merely sold through the Smith organisation.

Something of this sort seems to have occurred when they commercialised the type of pressed plant decoration which was once a craft for young ladies. At first the ferns were mounted directly on the wood and varnished over. Subsequently they were used as stencils in a form of spatterwork, the veining and other details being carefully painted in after the fern was removed. This fern ware seems to have been rather popular. Its production was finally mechanised and it has survived well. It was advertised in the Isle of Man from 1879 onwards. The pressed ferns and leaves, gathered on the Isle of Arran, were arranged as a collage and used to produce photographically an ornamental paper which could be applied to the ware in the same way as the tartans. Fern ware was made well into the twentieth century and, if instructions in craft books currently being sold bear fruit, is likely to be revived by the craft souvenir industry.

Other generalised souvenirs of Scotland were those commemorating Robert Burns, Sir Walter Scott and Bonnie Prince Charlie, all of which sold well and consistently. As has been indicated, Smiths' mechanised work was not wholly confined to souvenirs. They made patriotic items like the series of boxes started in 1841 which depicted Queen Victoria, and advertising packaging such as thread boxes and needle cases. Other firms did not always have the same diversity and thus did not last as long. The Pintos listed those known (in *Tunbridge and Scottish Woodware*) and the names of Daniel Eadie of Auchinleck, Thomas M'Millan of Cumnock, the partnership of Paterson & Lucas in Mauchline and George Dunlop and W.M. Lynn of Stewart Place, Catrine may be added. Much Scottish souvenir woodware survives, particularly the transfer-printed and tartan wares, and it is probably the most important category of wooden souvenir in the period under consideration.

TUNBRIDGE WARE

Tunbridge ware is now usually thought of as the distinctive end-grain wooden mosaic which was the usual form of woodware souvenir made in that spa throughout the nineteenth century and in the area, up to the outbreak of World War II. As with the Scottish snuffbox industry, a good deal of 'folk etymology' has circulated about the origins of the mosaic and its original manufacturer. When the spa first grew fashionable towards the end of the seventeenth century it became noted for fine wooden 'toys'. These were so popular that the manufacturers apparently had sales outlets in London. The firms followed contemporary fashions in furniture and interior decorating, including inlaid and painted finishes. At the beginning of the nineteenth century the Tunbridge Wells workshops were supplying souvenirs, already bearing the legend 'A present (or 'A trifle') from . . .' to nearby resorts such as Brighton and Margate. These seaside towns had already contrived to become popular, the former in the wake of the Prince Regent, the latter by virtue of the relatively easy travel afforded by the famous hoys. Much of the early work was turned but also included inlaid gaming boards and tea caddies and workboxes. At some time in the 1820s, a revolutionary process was devised for producing complicated geometric patterns in wood for use as veneers. This involved shaping an appropriate number of hardwood sticks and fastening them together so that their ends formed a pattern. The pattern was usually drawn out on squared paper first and closely resembled those used for Berlin woolwork. When the sticks had been glued together, they could be sliced as a single block and the slices used as veneers.

Plate 7 Tunbridge ware: note *A trifle from Margate* on the early painted piece (*left*).

The woods used were both imported and local and a variety of means was used to vary the normal colours. This included soaking wood such as bird's eye maple, holly or sycamore in the chalybeate spring water of the spa and selecting oak stained bright green by the fungus *Chlorociboria aeruginosum*. This fungus has tiny cup-shaped fruit bodies of the same improbably bright verdigris colour. The use of the fungus-stained wood in inlaid work was so well known that its scientific name in fact translates as 'green box'. It is likely that the earlier work has simpler patterns and that the large mosaics of roman-tic ruins and the wildlife designs are late. The range of products was considerable and quite large items of furniture continued to be made – the town was noted for its more simply inlaid furniture in the eight-eenth century – usually to a commission. As an alternative to cutting the glued block, it might be turned to produce a pattern by varying the depth of cutting. This is known as stickware and similar work is still produced abroad but with much coarser individual sticks.

It is difficult to say how many firms actually produced Tunbridge ware as they were certainly scattered over much of south-east England and they may well have existed further afield. Of the more important, Fenner & Nye of Tunbridge Wells, traded jointly and then split into two independent concerns. The Nye branch was succeeded by Thomas Barton. There were about a dozen other firms in the spa including Boyce, Brown & Kemp, who traded as Tunbridge Wells Manufacturing Co until about 1927. The trade was finally taken up by Thomas Lyttleton Green at Rye from 1931–9, but the destruction of his workshops, among other factors, prevented any postwar continuation. Wise's of Tonbridge have some claim, fostered by variable spellings of placenames (even the catalogue of the Great Exhibition has Tunbridge and Tonbridge Wells on successive lines), to have been innovators in woodware. They supplied smallware, particularly boxes, labelled 'A present from . . .' to many resorts and must have been one of Smith's of Mauchline's main competitors. James Medhurst of Weymouth, like Stiven's, specialised in association pieces, usually with a florid account of the wrecks, which had ostensibly provided the timber, as part of the design. However, it must be remembered that such pieces were also popular with amateur craftsmen and are still being made, often for fund-raising purposes. Medhurst worked about 1846–70. Small items in Tunbridge ware, both mosaic and the often earlier geometric veneer, are still quite common but the price of good pieces, particularly of less common types or those with elaborate or uncommon designs, is increasing. The simpler boxes might almost be described as plentiful but are still not as common as those in Mauchline transfer-printed ware. The Pinto collection in the City of Birmingham Museum has examples of most types of souvenir woodware.

FOREIGN WOODWARE

Small woodware items were among the usual stock of seaside bazaars, and would range from eastern bamboo to the traditional products of

Spa. At least six firms from this town exhibited at the Great Exhibition, doubtless partly in the hope of increasing their exports. Other exhibitors included Feistel & Sons of Aue near Scheeberg who offered Scottish boxes – presumably with integral hinges – a reminder that versions of the transfer-printed Mauchline ware and small wooden trinkets with porcelain topographical plaques were also made in Germany. Peasant woodware, including bent wood, birch bark and stave-built and turned containers, both plain and elaborately decorated, was and is freely imported from northern and central Europe and Russia.

THE CONTINUING TRADITION

After an eclipse of some thirty years, wooden souvenirs are again becoming fashionable. The relatively simple equipment required for turnery has attracted young independent craftsmen and turned wooden bowls, spoons, etc are widely sold. In general, the woods used are imported hardwoods but some workers use a high proportion of local timbers. Reproductions of butter moulds and prints,

Plate 8 Modern wooden souvenirs: Welsh love spoons designed and made by Ieuan Evans.

and other useful items for the kitchen, are popular. Joined items are less common, presumably because they are difficult for small workshops to produce economically. There are also a number of sculptors in wood, including a few from the traditional wood carving districts of the continent, catering largely for the tourist trade.

Wooden jewellery also is reappearing. Some pieces widely available are rather plain, relying on the colour and texture of selected timber for their aesthetic appeal. Others, particularly the bangles and beads of the hippie style, have the gaudy appeal of pseudo-primitives. More enterprising craftsmen are making better quality jewellery. Sometimes local woods appear in good settings, as in the blackthorn jewellery made by Kay and Peter Norris of Hawick. Hugh Kerr of Glenlivet has evolved what is virtually a new type of Scottish souvenir woodware. Small bundles of mature heather stems are put together, in a manner resembling Tunbridge stickware, and the polished cross sections are mounted in cross sections of staghorn. The resulting abstract patterns, mainly in yellows, reds and browns, set off by the plain white of the horn, are mounted in a variety of simple findings. Carved wooden jewellery remains uncommon and is virtually confined to simple bird and fish shapes.

A limited amount of Irish bog oak is still fashioned into the traditional harps and shamrocks, but the elaborate motifs have been largely superseded by slight surface ornament. To survive under modern conditions woodworkers have to concentrate on items simple to produce and finish or of such high quality that they command a commensurate price. Nevertheless, the now traditional blackthorn stick, 'emblem of the land of the shamrock and the shillelagh' as a Manx newspaper described it in 1840, still sells. Irish woodwork of quality is offered both by craftsmen working virtually alone, like Al O'Dea of Tuam, and alongside other goods, as at Abbeyleix where wood grown on the estate is turned into bowls and platters.

3 Souvenirs Made from Natural Materials

BASKETRY AND RUSHWORK

In the eighteenth and early nineteenth centuries most areas had their own local forms of containers for produce. It is not surprising that in those areas where suitable materials were particularly abundant such containers should be offered also to visitors. Thus picnic and fishing baskets of Somerset willow would be purchased by visitors to Glastonbury or Wells. Beautifully worked basket handbags were made in those areas which traditionally produced straw plait for hats, and were doubtless sold in country markets. However, most of the fancy baskets which formed part of the stock of the nineteenth century bazaars and fancy repositories were exotic. Baskets are surprisingly durable but, save where family tradition has recorded the origin of a workbasket or handbag, there is no means of identifying souvenirs as such. It appears that the addition of resort names in coloured raffia did not occur until after 1918 – it also enjoyed a revival in the late 1940s when souvenirs of any sort were hard to produce – and the substitution of Blackpool or Pwllheli for Madeira, in the coloured wool embroidery on baskets of the type characteristic of that island, is a phenomenon of the 1960s.

Basketry and rushwork were among the traditional crafts fostered by the Rural Industries Bureau (now CoSIRA) and similar bodies, workshops being set up in many tourist centres. The rush used is normally the true bulrush, *Scirpus lacustris*. Mats in various sizes, from table to room size, baskets, and a variety of more or less useful objects such as table napkin rings and covered glass containers for use as vases have become a standard part of the stock of craft gift shops even in districts where the reeds are not abundant and the raw materials have to be imported. The twin crafts are suitable also for handicapped workers, particularly the blind, and the products of sheltered workshops may also be offered in the tourist market. A further related craft is the making of corn dollies. Once objects of superstitious significance in preserving the fertility of the fields, then symbols hallowed by tradition in the agricultural community in certain areas, their status has dwindled to that of clever craft objects to demonstrate to Women's Institutes, or to mere souvenirs. Moreover, they are offered for sale in localities where they were not traditional. Other items of straw plait-work are made, such as ornaments which are ostensibly those worn at hiring fairs. Figures based on European peasant traditions are offered in gift shops, side by side with bird mobiles in rushwork imported from Taiwan and figures made from sugar cane or corn-on-the-cob leaves from equally far afield.

Irish basketry and rushwork

Basketry and rushwork have been fostered in Ireland as craftwork. Typical products are those of the Slievebawn co-operative markets, Roscommon, made for the tourist trade. Much of the Irish work is indistinguishable from English but there are some distinctive shapes based on those traditionally used in the countryside. These include simple chairs with seats of traditional straw rope, *sugan*, miniature creels and panniers. The latter are frequently offered, filled with peat, on a model of a donkey. The traditional symbol of the St Brigid's cross of rushes has also been revived. This was fashioned of reeds and placed on display to protect against evil during the coming year. The traditions and shapes varied from area to area but the crosses were usually made on St Brigid's day, 1 February. Each member of the

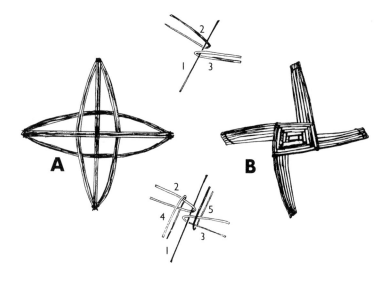

St Bridgid's crosses. To make type B, take three reeds and use one as a foundation (1). Bend the other two (2 and 3) in half and loop them over the foundation. Bend two more (4 and 5) and loop them over 2 and 3 so that they lie parallel to the foundation. This forms a basic cross. Continue to loop bent reeds over the cross, working around it until the desired size is reached. Tie off ends of arms and trim them.

household would sometimes make one, and in some areas a different shape was used for the stable, the byre and the dwelling house. The simplest forms, one of which is used by the Irish Television Service as its emblem, are fashioned entirely from rushes. More elaborate and decorative examples are worked over sticks fastened together in a cross shape, and there may be many diamonds on a single basic cross. Examples seen now are usually presented with a printed explanation of the tradition but the author has also been offered them, frequently made on the spot, by enterprising country children.

43

CORKWORK, COLLAGES, WALL PLAQUES AND SIMILAR ITEMS

Victorian parlours were decorated with other examples of the ingenious use of natural materials in addition to the 'flowers of the sea'. These might be purchased, or the work of ladies of the household, utilising souvenirs of their seaside holidays or local materials, like the coloured sands of Alum Bay, bought from enterprising traders. These set pieces might be three-dimensional. Such bouquets of shell or feather flowers, or scenes, would be displayed under glass domes known as shades, which has preserved many of them for posterity.

Corkwork

Pictures sculpted from cork were sold as souvenirs in the nineteenth century. A few, notably the elaborate views of Osborne House or Belvoir Castle, entailed so much skilled handwork that they must have been expensive. They are reminiscent of the finest Tunbridge perspective mosaics in style but are clearly later in date. The views are usually mounted in shallow boxes with elaborate glazed frames but rarely bear a significant signature. A variety of cork curiosities, such as model umbrellas, were sold in the Isle of Wight as having been made of cork from the Osborne cork oaks. These are known in fact to have been produced in Portugal. Most of the pictures of Osborne, and other architectural scenes, may therefore be of foreign origin. It is difficult to believe that they are not the work of professional craftsmen since they exist in such numbers. Similar work was, and is, certainly done in Japan but the subjects are now generally eastern in feeling.

More unsophisticated cork pictures, and cork items such as inkwells, were probably made by seasonal workers in what would otherwise have been workless winters. The pictures often have the university-style frame which, since it does not require mitred corners, is fairly easy for untrained woodworkers to make. The frames might be complicated with velvet insets, or embellished with shellwork.

Cork floats would provide a source of raw materials. Like building up models from matchsticks, cork sculpture was a popular hobby and it is a mistake to assume that all cork pictures were souvenirs or commercial products. Cork might be used in conjunction with a tinted print to produce a wall plaque, and also in the popular Victorian pastime of making what would now be called collages.

Collages

Despite the difficulties of working with nineteenth century glues, very attractive effects were obtained. Sand, rock fragments, twigs, bark, nuts, marine life and dried flowers and grasses were pressed, sometimes literally, into service to create landscapes. Architectural subjects such as churches were popular, probably because their definite outlines could easily be copied from a photograph. Delightful notes of fantasy creep in, such as the sleeping tabby cats fashioned from the striped coils of land snails.

When virtually identical scenes occur, such as Kirk Braddan church in the Isle of Man, they are likely to have been made in the locality for sale to visitors on a fairly regular basis. However, it seems that mass-production had to await the development of modern glues. North America has, as with other developments in the semi-craft souvenir industry, been the chief innovator. Aided by the great variety of suitable nuts and seed pods, a considerable industry has developed, producing wall plaques, table centres and similar novelties as well as framed collages and dried arrangements. Since the ingredients are cheap and easy to manipulate it is not surprising that British semi-commercial souvenir workers have taken up the making of similar pieces. In Victorian times, collage workers attracted admiration for their ingenuity. More recently, their medium has come to be regarded as 'legitimate' and the work of some artists commands the prices of native luxury goods and not mere souvenirs. Few early collages are signed and scenes are not always identifiable. Careful study may make it possible to localise part of the constituent wildlife which should afford some clue as to the place of origin.

HORN AND ANTLER SOUVENIRS

Cow horns and deer antler had been worked into useful items from the earliest times. Those commonly produced in the eighteenth and nineteenth centuries include buttons, combs and pins for the hair, combs for working butter in the dairy, drinking vessels, netting needles, spoons and scoops for household or shop use, snuff boxes and tatting shuttles. A wide range of antler souvenirs has been offered, mostly made on a large scale and covering sticks, with more or less elaborately worked handles, and toggle buttons to the highly finished napkin-rings, egg cups, spoons and ornaments of the modern Highland craft industries. Nineteenth century examples are generally more heavily ornamented and often have bejewelled silver mounts. Deer hoof souvenirs were made in Killarney but examples have not yet been identified.

Plate 9   Fine hornwork from the Abbey Horn Works, Kendal, Cumbria.

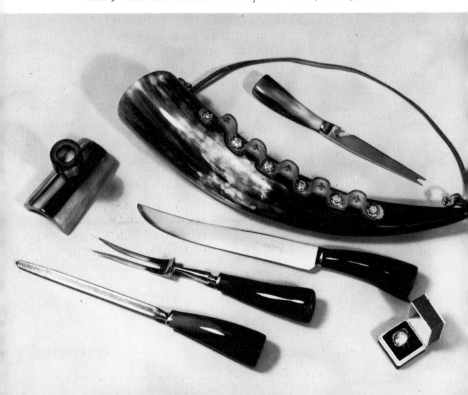

Cow horn souvenirs seem to have been less widely commercialised. The traditional beaker-shaped horn mug early became a souvenir by the addition of the magic words 'A present from . . .' – Aberystwyth, in the two examples dating from the 1890s known to the author. Snuff boxes and tatting shuttles were the other traditional wares occasionally offered as souvenirs. In recent years, pseudo-scrimshaw work in horn, mainly penguins and other birds with suitable silhouettes, and sailing vessels, has been imported in quantity and, in some instances, localised. The pedestrian quality of these imports becomes obvious if they are compared with the superb products of the long-established Abbey Horn Works at Kendal, where the silky lustre of the horn is fully exploited.

SEAWEED ALBUMS AND PICTURES

It is alleged that the earliest preserved English seaweed album is one made by Queen Victoria before her accession. The majority of those surviving are of considerably later date and reflect both the development of the science of marine biology and the Victorian interest in 'improving' hobbies for the young. Ornamental albums, with home-made twin card covers painted to resemble scallop shells and fastened with ribbons, were doubtless filled on wet days as a present for stay-at-home relations. They are holiday souvenirs in the same sense as snapshots. Instructions on how to mount seaweeds are given in innumerable popular books; for example, Rev J.G. Wood's *The Common Objects of the Sea Shore*, Routledge, Warne, and Routledge, London, 1864.

If the naturalist wishes to dry and preserve the algae which he finds, he may generally do so without much difficulty, although some plants give much more trouble than others. It is necessary that they should be well washed in fresh water, in order to get rid of the salt, which being deliquescent, would attract the water on a damp day, or in a damp situation, and soon ruin the entire collection.

When they are thoroughly washed the finest specimens should be separated from the rest, and placed in a wide, shallow vessel, filled with clean fresh water. Portions of white card, cut to the requisite size, should then be slipped under the specimens, which can be readily arranged as they float over the submerged card. The fingers alone ought to answer every purpose, but a camel's hair brush and a needle will often be useful. When the specimen is properly arranged, the card is lifted from the water, carrying upon it the piece of seaweed.

This author recommends 'the gelatine obtained by boiling the carrageen' when sufficient natural 'gelatinous substance' was not present to fasten the seaweed to the card. Virtually identical instructions are given by later authors, such as Johann Nave (in *The Collector's Handybook of Algae*, translated by Rev W.W. Spicer, George Routledge & Sons, London, 1904) and in fact are still repeated in modern instructions for naturalists.

From the 1860s, albums with covers elegantly blocked in gold with a title such as 'Flowers of the sea from Mona's Isle' were sold by seaside stationers and printers. Seaweeds also could be purchased already mounted on cards cut to fit the openings in the album mounts. These might be particularly attractive specimens, or groups of specimens, to enhance a young lady's reputation in selecting artistic arrangements for her album, or scientifically named examples to aid the budding naturalist in identification or to complete a collection from a particular locality. Herbarium sheets were also bound to order, sometimes after the holidaymaker had returned to his home town. Albums might be presented to a seaside hostess as a token of a guest's gratitude. Albums have survived in small numbers and most museums have a few examples, often included in herbaria. Specimen sheets prepared for sale survive less commonly in isolation, although the Manx Museum has a number collected by one of the staff of a Douglas draper about 1867, presumably to earn some small payment. The group was probably kept by him to facilitate identification of those mounted for sale. The individual cards, about 4in by 2½in, have borders ruled in red ink and are identical with those found in contemporary albums. Labelling is usually hand done in black, but printed slips cut from checklists are also known, together with purple ruled borders. As yet there is no sign of a revival of this particular collecting hobby except by naturalists interested in marine algae.

Dried seaweeds were also used ornamentally. Seaweed 'pictures', with a wreath of flowers rising from a basket to frame a suitable marine print and the inevitable verse 'O call us not weeds, we are flowers of the sea . . . ' and the legends 'A present from . . . ' or 'Flowers of the sea from . . . ' are quite common. They are usually in rather deep frames, either gilt or maple wood, and frequently oval. Inspection will often show that the remains of sea mats and small shells are included also. Advertisements make it clear that such items were produced for sale although the ingredients could no doubt be purchased by the amateur craftswomen. As late as 1882, 'Isabella Johnson Printer, Bookseller and Stationer' of Douglas was still offering 'A choice Selection of MANX SEAWEEDS neatly mounted on cardboard In various devices . . . ', and seaweed-decorated novelties were still being made at the beginning of the twentieth century. In recent years they have begun to share the vogue for 'pressed flower pictures', seaweeds appearing as part of the furnishings in 'underwater scenes', or simple patterns of natural objects, embedded in plastic. (At the end of the nineteenth century, Smith's of Mauchline commercialised a related pressed plant craft in their Fern ware.)

'Flowers of the sea' verses from seaweed pictures

Mona's Sea Weeds

1. O call us not weeds, we are flowers of the sea
   For lovely, and gay, and bright-tinted are we,
   Our blush is as deep as the rose of thy bower,
   Then call us not weeds, we are ocean's gay flowers.

2. Not nursed like the plants of the summer parterre,
   Whose gales are but sighs of the evening air,
   Our exquisite fragrance, and delicate forms,
   are the prey of the ocean, when vexed with the storms.

3. And thus 'tis in life, like weeds thrown away,
   As many who bask not in fortune's bright ray,
   Whose sunshine of life would shed lustre round,
   And in weal, or woe, brightly tinted be found.

Manx Museum collection

Variant 1: verse 1 alone, same title, Manx Museum collection

Variant 2: unlocalised, signed E.K. Giesbach, 1850, private collection
   verse 1 line 1, initial O omitted
        line 2, bright and gay transposed
        line 3, And quite independent of sunshine and showers
   verse 2 line 3, Our delicate, fragile and exquisite forms
        line 4, Are nurs'd by the billows, and rock'd by the storms

SHELLS AND SHELLWORK

Early history

Shells were one of the first durable natural objects to be collected. Initially they may have had a magical significance to augment their attractiveness as ornaments. Sea shells painted in brilliant colours were among the sacred objects found in the Middle Minoan 'temple repositories' of the palace of Minos at Knossos in Crete. Ornaments made from the thorny oyster (*Spondylus gaederopus*) were widely traded in prehistoric Europe while those made from the Indian chank (*Turbinella pyrum*) reached as far as ancient Mesopotamia. The latter shell still has a religious significance in India. Trumpets made from chank are blown on propitious occasions and a pair of lacquered chank bangles serve as a Hindu bride's 'wedding ring'. The scallop was a symbol of pilgrimage, specifically to the shrine of St James at Compostella in Spain, by the twelfth century. From the evidence of an ordinance of Charles VI of France, issued in 1393, scallop shells were also sold to pious visitors to Mont St Michel. The most common lead pilgrim's badge produced for this shrine also showed scallops, with a figure of St Michael.

Exotic shells have nearly as long a history as souvenirs in their own right. Textile cones, eroded and panther cowries and a pearl shell (*Conus textile, Cypraea erosa, C. pantherina* and *Pinctada margaritifera*) were found by the excavators of Pompeii. These shells must have come from at least as far away as the Red Sea. By the seventeenth century the opening up of trade routes in tropical seas brought a wealth of vividly coloured and fantastically sculptured shells to Europe. These were collected, exchanged and sold by those with scientific curiosity. Even a common Mediterranean species such as the fan mussel, and fabric woven from its byssus, excited the interest of John Evelyn, and examples of this and similar curiosities doubtless came to Britain as souvenirs of many later grand tours.

Shellwork

As well as being adornments to more or less scientific collections, shells were fashioned into ornaments. In view of the cheapness of the basic materials it is not surprising that shellwork novelties have held their own and are still produced, particularly by the semi-amateur and cottage industry souvenir workshops. One of the older forms of shellwork is the attachment of small shells to a ground, such as a box or mirror frame. Skilled Victorian exponents produced sets of hanging shelves, complete chimney pieces and large grottos, but these were hardly souvenirs unless the shells were collected personally. Smaller items were produced for the souvenir trade. A certain uniformity of execution and materials may sometimes betray this commercial work. Local British shells were used but imported species,

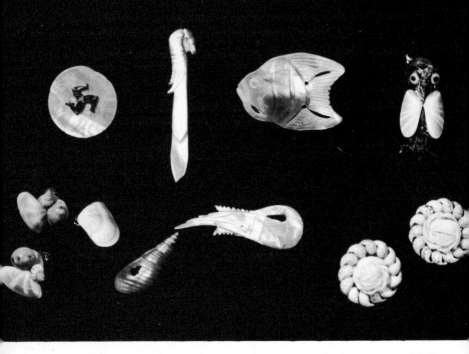

Plates 10–11 These twentieth-century pieces illustrate the diverse origins of shells used by the souvenir manufacturers. *Above:* (1) 1890s pearl shell brooch with blue enamelled three-legs emblem, possibly Japanese, (2) Bookmark of pearl shell in shape of shrimp, 1920s, origin unknown, (3) Fish brooch of cut abalone shell, Taiwan, (4) Owl brooch with tellin shell wings, cone scale body, cup shell eyes, USA, (5 and 6) Earrings of European cowrie, thick-lipped dogwhelk, and tellin, one with pendant, 1950s, UK, (7) Pearly shell, pierced for suspension, possibly Australian, (8) Brooch of stained pearl shell in shape of shrimp, 1920s, origin unknown, (9) Earrings of cup shells surrounded by nerites, possibly North America. *Right:* (1) Frog figure; serpent cowrie body, *Cerithium* legs, star limpet hands and feet, carpet shell head, Far East, possibly Taiwan or Japan, (2) Paperweight of ormer and crab embedded in plastic, 1960s, Hong Kong, (3) Dish of pearl shell cut to shape of fish, Pacific area, possibly Philippines, (4) Cat figure, cut scallop shells, and (5) Shell box, both modern, Isle of Man, (6 and 7) Vases for miniature flower arrangements, hairy whelk and mount of paired trough shells, 1930s, Australia.

particularly small pearly tops – dyed in later examples – and white
'rice grains', are also commonly met with. The shells were often
mounted in a paste which was soft when fresh but dried hard to hold
them firmly in position. An interesting sidelight on the Victorian shell
souvenir trade is the fact that the eponymous shell was selected as the
badge of the Shell Transport & Trading Company because shell ornaments were so important a part of the stock of Marcus Samuel senior,
father of the company's founders, Marcus and Samuel. Examples of
ornaments decorated with shells (not localised) sold by M. Samuel
and Son are displayed in the Shell Building, South Bank, London and
others are preserved by the Bethnal Green Museum, London (a
branch of the Victoria and Albert Museum). The latter were lent to
the South Kensington Museum in 1857. The museum also has a few

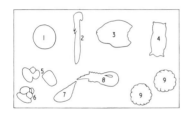 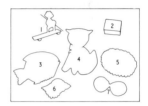

later pieces purchased from Messrs P.L. Simmonds in 1875 but in neither case is it possible to know whether the items were made in Britain or abroad. The Samuel ornaments at the Victoria and Albert Museum incorporate dyed shells and in some cases they are mounted on cardboard, not wood, indicating that this is not exclusively a twentieth century economy in making shell boxes. Most early shell ornaments are varnished.

In recent years, a related hobby has developed based on modern materials. Glass bottles for use as lamp bases, flower pots, preserve and paste jars, etc are encrusted with shells set in the quick drying cellulose filler used for patching walls when decorating. This is preferred to barbola paste and similar mediums because it is stored dry. Where they are abundant, flat winkles, preferably yellow or orange, are favoured. Commercial firms often incorporate exotic or dyed material and produce markedly patterned designs, with bands of different species such as mussels and pelican's foot shells. This sort of shellwork is also popular for fund raising purposes. More traditional methods are used to decorate coloured card boxes, mirror frames, vases and boxes for cheap musical box movements.

Shells might be fashioned into practical items, as well as the purely ornamental. Pincushions were often made locally in seaside resorts. There are two types. In one, the pad into which the pins are stuck is housed in the mouth of a large coiled shell such as a whelk or a limpet 'dish', the whole being mounted on shell feet. Alternatively, paired bivalves (the type of shell known in the USA as a clam), might be joined over the pad, often by means of lacing through holes drilled in the edges of the twin shells. Small pink 'queenie' scallops were particularly popular for these but large cockles might also be used. Both types may carry painted inscriptions. (The Bethnal Green Museum has examples, dating from 1875.) 'A present from Snowdon' of the 1880s is a commercial variant of the scallop pincushion, with cut pearl shell used as the outside of a purse. The half shell shapes are attached to a metal frame by means of scarlet material. The frame, about 2in wide by 1½in deep, closes with two metal knobs and two inner compartments are fashioned from scarlet cardboard. The black lettering, on one side only, is accompanied by a garland of three pink flowers and green leaves. Similar pieces were sold, more appropriately, at the seaside. As with most souvenirs, such shellwork seldom bears any real indication of origin. Printed labels sometimes exist but are more frequently those of the retailer or wholesaler than the maker. It would seem that made-up shell novelties were imported from the Far East from the very beginnings of the trade.

Early shellwork plaques and boxes are becoming less common as their popularity with collectors increases. They seldom survive in good condition. If not heavily varnished they are often impossible to clean, while if well coated the discoloured varnish will equally spoil their appearance. Groups of shells stripped to reveal their inner nacreous layers have often fared better. In the late Victorian period, it was common to strip shells for display in this way – modern collectors prefer to preserve as far as possible the appearance of the living creature. There is a particularly fine exhibit of such stripped shells in the Guille Alles Museum in St Peter Port, Guernsey, Channel Islands. Shells which are not mounted can be washed in tepid soapy water, bleached quickly in a weak solution of household bleach if necessary, and their appearance restored with a light rub with a mineral oil – not animal or vegetable as this would become rancid. However, care should be taken that important scientific material is not so treated. Locality labels may indicate origin, and a value beyond that of simple souvenirs of happy days on the shore.

Shellwork flowers and figures

Elaborate floral bouquets have often survived because they are kept under glass shades. Shell-flower making was an elegant eighteenth century pastime which was widely revived during the period 1840–65. Most examples date from the later period.

The rising popularity of shellwork novelties with semi-amateur souvenir makers in the twentieth century reflects the immense improvement in the quality and ease of use of the glues available. Since the 1920s, every seaside shop has offered scallop shells mounted on smaller species to make ash or pin trays, penguins with mussel shell wings, crinoline ladies with tiered skirts of graduated limpet shells, and similar examples of skill and ingenuity. Books of instruction abound and suggested groupings are often illustrated in girls' annuals and hobby books. At their best they are extremely entertaining, but when overmuch colouring and varnishing obscures the basic attractiveness of the raw materials they can be ugly. Imported shellwork novelties, mainly from Taiwan and other eastern sources, occur with increasing frequency. These include sawn tiger cowries (also worked in Britain) and ships with cockle shell sails, seemingly an imitation of early scrimshaw work vessels.

Sailors' gifts

Other exotic shellwork brought in during the nineteenth century notably includes sailors' valentines. These take the form of glazed wooden frames containing richly patterned arrangements of small brightly-coloured shells and, occasionally, seed pods. The frames are often six or eight sided and may be hinged together in pairs. Complete table tops are also known. Examples marked 'A present from Barbados' survive but similar collections were made on other West Indian islands. Unglazed boxes of shells and seeds, with similar internal partitions were put together in India (the Manx Museum has an example made in Bombay about 1910) and, one suspects, for Port Said dealers. As far as is known, these pieces were imported individually as sailors' or tourists' gifts and not on a commercial scale.

Shellwork jewellery

Suitable shells have been carved into cameos and irridescent mother-of-pearl has formed part of a jeweller's stock-in-trade since earliest times, but shell jewellery of a less precious character is a fairly recent innovation. In the Victorian period, shells instead of polished beach pebbles were linked with simple silver mounts to make chains and bracelets, but this was uncommon. Most of the strings of winkles, heavily varnished to restore their sea-wet appearance, belong to the craze for jewellery made from natural objects which flourished on the fringes of the 'arts and crafts' movement from about 1910 onwards.

Shell jewellery had a certain added impetus in the period 1939–45 when imported raw materials were not available to hobbyists. As late as 1951 a booth at the Battersea Pleasure Gardens of the Festival of Britain offered instruction in piercing shells, and sold the necessary findings for mounting the results. At about the same period, 'artistic' as opposed to novelty shell jewellery enjoyed something of a vogue in North America. Tiny shells, often dyed, and garfish scales were fashioned into delicate floral designs and resort shops offered raw materials, often as kits including instructions, as well as the finished ornaments. The delicate lacework produced by sawing the elegant turrets of wentletraps lengthwise is one of the hallmarks of shell jewellery at this period. It is uncommon in British products and it seems that dollar restrictions made it impossible for shops to import American raw materials consistently. More recently, controls on currency for the purchase of exotic shells and fads for natural materials has increased the popularity of necklaces, pendants, bracelets and belts made from local shells, and the profitability of workshops making them. They are now one of the standard seaside souvenirs, together with shellwork musical boxes, plant pots and varnished view plaques framed in rings of pearly tops.

Embedding in plastic

Modern plastic resins and fibreglass technology have given rise to a new craft: embedding objects in clear or tinted plastic. This first reached the souvenir market and subsequently the amateur in North America, where advertisements for home kits appeared in the late 1950s. Shells are particularly popular as, unlike pressed flowers and dried butterflies, they seldom give rise to problems with air bubbles. They may be arranged in patterns or as natural scenes. According to the size of the mount, the finished model may be anything from a bookend or television light to earrings or the pendant for a keyring. The range made from items (leaves, seeds, flowers, ferns, dead insects and fishing flies are but a few) embedded in plastic is enormous and forms part of the trend towards natural souvenirs.

4 Geological Souvenirs

EARLY HISTORY

The collection of geological specimens, whether ordinary rock samples, fine examples of minerals, or fossils, was one of the pastimes popular with holidaymakers before they were provided with more contrived entertainment. Like botany and conchology, geology is given due attention by early guide books. Some areas were particularly noted for their fossils, for example Lyme Regis, Freshwater, Harwich, Holderness and Hornsea. The last two were noted by Sir George Head in his *Home Tour*, published by John Murray in 1841. He indicates that a few local people were already offering fossils for sale and also alludes to the carefully contrived curiosities (such as an artificial nest, with eggs twined with ivy) that were placed in the spring at Matlock to be coated with a limy deposit before being sold to visitors, 'petrifactions also, similar but superior to those at the dripping-well at Knaresborough'.

ALUM BAY AND SANDWORK

Just as the Victorians were attracted by the simple curiosities produced by the petrifying springs at Matlock and Knaresborough (a table fashioned from stalagmites from the latter appeared in the Great Exhibition) so they enjoyed the novelty of a glass vial filled with the different shades of sand from the coloured cliffs at Alum Bay in the Isle of Wight. In Mavor's *The British Tourists*, published in 1798, the white sand and coloured strata at Alum Bay are mentioned but more space is devoted to the shepherd boys sliding down the steep grass slopes of St Boniface Down. 'For their amusement, or a trifling reward, they will seat themselves on a horse's headbone, and steer themselves down the steepest declivities with incomparable art and velocity.' However, fifty years later visitors were told that there were at least twelve different shades of sand 'coloured like the finest silk' and invited to purchase a glass vessel in which to accumulate the pattern of their choice. Alternatively, they could buy a vase or pair of urns already filled. Shapes more or less follow contemporary fashions in mantel ornaments but straight-sided columns like laboratory containers and 'lighthouses' were also popular. Usually, the sand forms horizontal stripes.

Quite elaborate pictures were made. Those for the souvenir trade usually depict an Isle of Wight view but the making of sand pictures, and the use of sand in making what now would be called collages, were popular Victorian pastimes which are currently being revived. Sand and other materials were glued to a background, often a printed scene, and the result would be framed and glazed. Alum Bay sands were sold in small packets for hobbyists to make their own designs. Isle of Wight sand from related but less vividly coloured strata elsewhere in the island was also sold and ostensibly formed an ingredient of Isle of Wight sand soap, shown at the Great Exhibition.

Coloured sands were used to fill clear glass containers which had been decorated by sticking cutouts or scraps of printed paper to the inner surface. This Victorian hobby, which lasted from about 1855–1905, although occasional later pieces do occur, was known as potichomania. The use of the sand filling ensured, as the more usual opaque paint does not, that the owner was not tempted to arrange flowers in water in the vase. Thus sand-filled potichomania vases are often well preserved. Inevitably some vases are inscribed 'A present from . . .', or their decoration has a nautical flavour. Examples made at home from bought sand may also have a patriotic motif, commemorations of Queen Victoria's Jubilee being so common as to hint that some popular magazine suggested this idea.

Alum Bay sand glasses have had a surprisingly long-lasting popular appeal for so unsophisticated a souvenir. Their popularity weathered two world wars and the present Main Bazaar near the Needles Hotel still offers 'sand pictures and shaped bottles and tubes filled with the coloured sand'. Moreover, it still faces competition from neighbouring deposits of Isle of Wight sand. The shapes still include lighthouses. One wonders why the Isle of Wight, like the Isle of Man, should have developed and largely retained so wide a range of uniquely local souvenirs.

CONNEMARA MARBLE

A similar stone to the distinctive apple-green Iona marble was located in the area between the new town of Clifden and Galway and used extensively to make Irish exhibits for the Great Exhibition of 1851. These were mainly large pieces such as urns, tables and ornamental

Plate 12 (1) Derbyshire alabaster dish, (2) Engraved glass, and (3) its late Mauchline ware box, with photographic view on lid, (4) Portsoy marble vase of Ancient Egyptian shape.

panels. Very good examples of the latter adorn the staircase of the Geological Museum, South Kensington, London but, like the Derbyshire stonework also shown in this museum, are outside the scope of this book. The panels came from the Ballynahinch quarry. Latterly, other quarries have been opened at Cregs and Streamstown, north of Clifden, and Bunowen, Glendnagh and Recess to the east. Their products are used mainly for personal ornaments (cufflinks, tie pins and tacks, rings, brooches, etc) but ash trays and small ornaments are made.

Unless the design involves shamrocks or Irish harps such pieces may be indistinguishable from those of Iona marble. Designs in Connemara jewellery follow contemporary fashion. In the Victorian period, small oblong harp and shamrock brooches, usually enriched with marcasite, are common. The 1920s produced debased Art Nouveau designs and, more recently, standard findings and mechanised stone cutting have taken over. However, some craftsmen still use Connemara marble, notably those whose products bear the shamrock mark of the Glencolumcille industry.

DERBYSHIRE STONE

During his visit to Derbyshire, Sir George Head observed that 'There are many rival shops, and exhibitions, or show-rooms, in the town of Matlock, all containing choice ornaments in spar and Derbyshire marble . . .' Local tradition now avers that the exploitation of the rich purple veining of the Derbyshire fluorspar, or Blue John, dates back to Roman times. The souvenir trade in spar and alabaster ornaments was certainly well established at the very beginning of the period under consideration. Britton and Brayley record in their *Beauties of England and Wales,* published in 1802, that at Matlock

The original silk mill . . . is at present in the occupation of Messrs. Brown & Son, who employ it for the cutting and polishing of marble, and manufacturing the Derbyshire fluorspar, or Blue John, and Gypsum, into a variety of beautiful ornaments, as urns, vases, columns, obelisks &c.

They also give a detailed description of the way in which the stone was worked.

When the Blue John is being made into a vase, or any other ornamental form that renders the use of the lathe necessary, it is carved with a mallet and chissel, into a rude resemblance of the object intended to be produced, and afterwards strongly cemented to a plug or *chock*, is screwed upon the lathe. A slow motion is then given to the work; and a bar of steel, about two feet long, and half an inch square, properly tempered, and pointed at each end, is applied to the fluor, on which water is continually dropping, to keep the tool cold, preserve it from friction, and enable it more readily to reduce the substance on which it acts. As the surface becomes smoother, the tool is applied with more freedom, and the motion of the lathe accellerated, till the fluor has assumed its destined elegance of form. When the turning is completed, pieces of grit-stone of different degrees of fineness, are applied with water to bring the article to a proper ground for polishing with fine emery, tripoli, and putty, or calx of tin. These means are continued till the fluor is incapable of receiving a higher degree of polish; which is known when water thrown on it will no longer increase its lustre.

(Original spelling retained.)

The stone used was obtained from quarries west of Castleton, which were open to visitors, for whom the guides would chip specimens of the native rock. The worked fluorspar was always expensive even after the use of water- rather than foot-powered lathes had reduced breakages. Nevertheless, it seems to have enjoyed a ready sale – the master bedroom of a house in Ramsey, Isle of Man had, according to a sale inventory of 1847, two Derbyshire spar candlesticks flanked by large ornamental sea shells. Superlative examples of turned

Blue John may be seen at Chatsworth and in the Geological Museum at South Kensington. The deposit was not inexhaustible and pieces suitable for making large ornaments are not now readily obtainable. In consequence, only jewellery is now being made in quantity.

The much more abundant alabaster was, and is, also worked on a lathe. The usual shapes are vaguely Italianate: urns, tazzas, rather heavy candlesticks and a variety of lidded boxes. The retail outlets spread over a number of towns and villages in the Buxton and Matlock area. In 1802 there were already:

> Several shops for the manufacture and sale of ornaments of fluorspar, and alabaster . . . established in the village. The most finished and best assortment of articles of this description are exhibited in the warehouse of Mr Samuel Cooper (at Buxton).

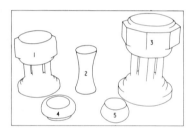

Plate 13 (1, 3, 4 and 5) Cornish 'marble', (2) Derbyshire alabaster vase.

The same enterprising traders offered minerals from the lead mines and specimens from the various 'marble' quarries, as well as fluorspar and fossils.

The 'marble' quarries had been developed under the auspices of the Duke of Devonshire who, in the eighteenth century, had encouraged workmen employed by Henry Watson of Bakewell to study the examples of Italian stone inlay at Chatsworth. In consequence, a local industry had developed producing mainly fireplaces and other architectural details, and furniture such as tables and benches, in the Italian manner. This was both bulky and costly and hardly catered for the souvenir trade save in the most grandiose tradition of the grand tour. At the beginning of the nineteenth century, the marble trade had declined and was mainly supplying, with the aid of a 'sweeping floor' at the Ashford works capable of polishing eighty square feet of surface at a time, plain panels. There was a revival later in the century and a number of firms exhibited elaborate inlaid tables and fireplaces at the Great Exhibition. At about this time, some of the workshops do seem to have made smaller items for the tourists. These include book ends, paperweights and mantel ornaments in the form of obelisks, in which the contrast between the mottled grey marble of Ricklow Dale near Monyash and Ashford black marble was exploited. Occasionally, small items might be inlaid. Since the author was offered as local work an oval brooch, inlaid with a floral design, by a shop at Matlock Bath in 1966, these may have included jewellery in the Italian *pietro dura* style. The clientèle for the large pieces was so restricted that the inlay workshops all closed by 1900.

CORNISH AND OTHER MARBLES AND SERPENTINES

By the mid-nineteenth century, Derbyshire's example in the exploitation of local rocks for the souvenir trade had been extensively followed. At the Great Exhibition of 1851 'the beautiful limestones of Derbyshire, and its fluor-spar, which have been by the ingenious workmen of that county, wrought into almost every form of article for house decoration' were joined by 'the less known, but even more beautiful serpentines of Cornwall and Ireland, of which are displayed obelisks, columns, candelabra and vases; the marbles of Devonshire, the porphyries and granites of Scotland, of Ireland, and of south-western England . . .' The serpentine marble works at Penzance were established about 1850 and similar items to those illustrated on p 64 were produced until the end of the century. After World War I they catered for 'modern tastes' and the Cornish stone souvenirs acquired new 'traditional' forms – a turned mushroom on which sits a lucky pixie, or a lump of serpentine labelled 'A present from . . .' and ornamented with a turned lighthouse (or, more recently and with cheaper items, a casting) and a seagull. Egg timers, thermometer mounts and the like appeared.

The Portsoy quarries in Banffshire were a source of 'marble' for architectural use. Some small items seem to have been produced quite early and in recent years an attractive range of pleasingly plain desk ornaments has been made. Usual items include pen stands, paper knife handles, book ends and weights. Since the stone is readily turned, highly polished ovoids abound together with more rectilinear shapes which exploit the contrast in colour between the deep grey-green of the polished surface and the lighter appearance of the unpolished. The Lintstone (Glasgow) factory of the Scottish Curling Stone Co produces similar items from waste, light green Ailsa Craig stone.

Few other stones have been worked consistently over a long period but many were utilised when stone souvenirs were economic to produce. This was chiefly during the Victorian period, when labour was cheap and the rather heavy products suited current styles of interior decorating. Much more recently, the spread of relatively inexpensive electric-powered lapidary equipment, initially from the USA, has encouraged the establishment of stonecraft workshops. Continuous production of geological souvenirs other than jewellery seems to have been confined to areas where there were large markets and the stone, such as Charnwood porphyry, Cornish serpentine or Derbyshire alabaster, was easily worked and in good supply.

5 Jewellery

GEOLOGICAL JEWELLERY

Samples collected on geological rambles were often turned into jewellery and items ostensibly made from local stones were popular souvenirs. The most important and longest-established English centre of production of geological jewellery was Whitby, where jet earlier attracted the attention of the Romans. The industry is alleged to have benefited from the period of mourning for William IV and by 1853 its annual value was said to be in the region of £20,000. Its popularity continued to increase for a time, partly as a result of Queen Victoria's influence, and there were some 200 workshops, with a combined turnover of £84,000, in 1870. Jet was turned and carved and considerable skill was needed in its working, so it is not surprising that attempts were made to copy its black gleam in materials that lent themselves more easily to mass production. Thus in an 1857 directory of Birmingham W. Willmott appears as a 'Black ornament manufacturer' offering 'Studs Bracelets Hoops Buckles Slides Brooches' and he was but one among many in England and on the continent. Partly as a result of changes in fashion and partly because of the multiplication of cheaper imitations, the Whitby industry declined. An 1895 guide book author could write 'Lately the trade has been much depressed'. The Whitby jewellery workshops operated on a large scale and their products were by no means exclusively souvenirs. Jet ornaments were sold widely in the British Isles and abroad and there were periods when they were fashionable. However, the last of the

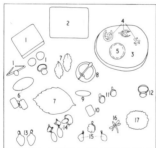

Plate 14 Jewellery: (1) Box from W. Smith, Matlock Bath, Derbyshire, with 1950s Blue John clip earrings and 1930s silver-set ring and malachite tiepin, (2) Scottish heather-stem brooch, set in stag-horn, 1972, (3) Scottish polished stone paperweight, (4) Silver three-legs brooches, 1890s, and advertising stick-pin, 1930s, (5) Silver brooch. 'Iona', marked JH, prob-ably 1930s, (6) Brooch in base metal setting, plain clip earrings, Connemara marble, 1960s, (7) Typical preserved leaf jewellery in copper – beech brooch, oak earrings, 1960s, Wales, (8) Scottish silver penannular brooch of type still made, (9) Art Nou-veau brooch, green enamel and silver, of type sold widely 1920–39, (10) Stainless steel ring with three-legs emblem, 1970s, (11) Silver-mounted screw earrings set with Iona marble, purchased Tiree 1960s, (12) Silver ring set with imported moss agate, purchased Tongue, Sutherland, 1972, (13) Metallic-glazed pottery earrings, Lyme Regis, 1950s, (14) Silver-mounted drop earrings and ring, marked HMJ and GCK in shamrock, Glencolumcille, Donegal, (15) Tumble-polished drops as sold throughout British Isles, 1960s on, (16) Dragonfly brooch, 1930s (17) Irish bog oak brooch, 1890s.

craftsmen in the old tradition died in 1932 and local shops now offer 'antique' pieces, or 'simulated jet'. Other east coast resorts offered jewellery allegedly made from local jet and the presence of jet pebbles, usually accompanied by amber, is one of the attractions noted in *Seaside Watering Places* in 1895, an indication of the length of time geological jewellery remained in vogue. Amber was used to a limited extent in souvenirs on the east coast. According to *Adam's Illustrated Descriptive Guide to the Watering Places* of 1848, Harwich made a speciality of translucent pebbles set as rings. By implication these were of local origin but, as with Messrs A. & M. Lemon's 'MANX PEBBLES in Brooches, Hearts, Crosses, and Seals, with the Arms of the Island, Specimens &c . . .' (1845) it is doubtful whether sufficient local raw materials of quality were available. Trifles made from coral, pearl, amber and jet (or imitations of them) were among the usual offerings of resort jewellers. To some extent this souvenir geological jewellery followed fashion. Lemon's subsequently added armlets, shawl pins, and brooches in the shape of an anchor to their range. Where semi-precious stones were really common there were usually working lapidaries willing to make up customers' finds, or sell finished pieces. Thus, at Sidmouth, 'There are scarcely any shells, but the pebbles are very good; many of jasper, agate, chalcedony and cornelian, are to be found, and at several shops in the town finished specimens may be bought, or those picked up polished and set'. Similarly at Budleigh Salterton '. . . fine specimens of moss agate and chalcedony are found here, and cut and polished in the village'. Further west, the 'crystal beach' at Marazion, opposite St Michael's Mount, like the islet itself, was noted for amethyst and citrine. Locations likely to yield semi-precious stones were long recorded in guide books but their importance in the souvenir trade declined in the first half of the twentieth century. However, inexpensive electric-powered tumblers arrived in the 1960s and there was a great upsurge of interest in native hard stones of attractive appearance. Generally, modern geological jewellery is of a poor technical standard, with a great reliance on uninteresting standard findings and the strength of modern adhesives. Nineteenth century pieces are more frequently in good quality settings with highly finished stones.

The author has seen few pieces set with colourless quartz although there are frequent literary references to Bristol, Buxton, Cornish, Irish, Isle of Wight or 'occidental' diamonds, and in Ireland Dungiven crystals are mentioned. It seems clear that glass 'brilliants' imported from the continent were used as well as the native quartz. Souvenir jewellery which followed fashion becomes indistinguishable from that produced for other outlets for inexpensive trifles. Unless the design is as firmly localised as a silver bar brooch with grey granite ends, lettered JERSEY, or the Manx three-legs, it is impossible to identify souvenirs. Irish shamrock and Scottish heather were sold elsewhere as good luck emblems. A competent jeweller can often indicate that the quality of stones is too high to be native but this does not preclude their having been sold as such. Regrettably few jewellers' catalogues of the nineteenth century have survived, so geological jewellery without a history can only have been collected as such, not as localised souvenirs. Nevertheless, such pieces are eminently collectable.

FRESHWATER PEARLS

The freshwater pearl mussel *Margaritifera margaritifera* was once so abundant in British rivers that the fine pearls it yielded are said to have been one of the treasures that lured Julius Caesar to Britain. Pollution, the damming of streams for power and, after the seventeenth century, the run-off from limed fields gradually reduced its range. The contraction was accelerated by the effects of the Industrial Revolution. Since it was necessary to kill the creature in order to discover whether pearls were present, destructive overfishing was also likely. Thus, although the Manx Museum has a fine pearl – one of a string subsequently mounted as a tiepin – from the River Dhoo, the pearl mussel apparently became extinct in Man by about 1870. A similar fate overtook the populations in many English rivers but profitable fisheries survived in Ireland, Scotland and Wales, pearls being drawn anew to the attention of the fashionable by the display at the 1851 Exhibition.

Traditionally some pearl mussel fisheries were restricted, but in other areas they were worked by transients such as gypsies, or by a few local people, who hawked their pearls to visitors or, particularly in the case of the finer examples, sold them to local jewellers. Pearls of good lustre and unusual colours did occur and sometimes reached distant markets, but after about 1850 most were sold in simple settings in the districts where they were collected. The interest in the native products of the British Isles aroused by preparations for the Great Exhibition may be seen from the fact that Cowie & Rae of Ellon in Scotland displayed pearls from the River Ythan in Aberdeenshire. In an 1837 directory, they are respectively a vintner and a grocer. The Ythan, together with the Don and the Ugie, also supplied G. Jamieson of 107 Union Street, Aberdeen with pearls to set round Cairngorms, a style often met with in Scottish jewellery.

J. Nelis of Omagh, Co Tyrone, provided a case of pearls 'found in the deepest part of the River Strule at Omagh, Ireland' and J. West & Son of Dublin offered 'Jewellery, embellished with Irish pearls and other gems . . .' It is extremely difficult to identify the origin of the pearls set in the numerous small brooches, suitable wear for young girls, that have survived from the Victorian period but, particularly when they accompany cairngorms or bog oak, they must frequently have been sold as the product of a local fishery. Some pearls were obtained in Wales. Overfishing and changes in fashion caused the eclipse of freshwater pearls although they still are widely sold in Scotland. Regrettably, many have all the attractiveness of tiny drops of solder and most of the settings are of poor quality. When a fine pearl is mounted by a craftsman, the final price of the piece may place it at the expensive end of the market but it may well prove as durable as those of the nineteenth century.

Pearls from the edible mussel *Mytilus edulis* were also in vogue in Victorian times, notably those from Conway, but were apparently too scarce to be the foundation of a lasting souvenir trade.

The first development of peculiarly Irish jewellery for the souvenir trade seems to have occurred between the accession of Queen Victoria and the Great Exhibition of 1851. There are three basic categories, which frequently overlap. Pieces are made from specifically Irish materials, such as Connemara marble or bog oak; there are those with 'typically Irish' motifs, such as harps and shamrocks; and revivals of older designs. The last range from the Claddagh rings, traditionally associated with Galway's harbour area where they were said to have been worn to ensure the identification of drowned sailors, to fine reproductions of Celtic jewellery such as the 'Royal Irish Tara Brooch' exhibited at the Great Exhibition by 'Waterhouse & Co, The Queen's Silversmith, of 25 Dame Street, Dublin'. More recently, there has been a revival of enamel work using ancient patterns and much attractive craft jewellery has appeared.

Irish brooches shown at the Great Exhibition, London, 1851. Waterhouse & Co (a–d), West (e).

Plate 15 A set in 'Irish diamonds' by Goggin & Co, Dublin; harp and shamrock motifs. Late nineteenth century.

Not surprisingly, the main concentration of jewellers offering souvenirs was in Dublin, to judge from directories and advertisements. Among the more noteworthy firms were Cornelius and Jeremiah Goggin, of 13 Nassau Street and 74 Grafton Street respectively. The City Museum and Art Gallery at Birmingham has a charming parure of iron pyrites mounted in silver made by the latter, still with its original case marked 'Goggin & Company, Grafton Street, Dublin, Irish bog oak carvers to Her Majesty'. The drop earrings consist of five-petalled flowers but the bracelet, brooch and necklace have a shamrock motif, the two last with pendant Irish harps. It is believed that this piece was made as early as the 1840s, since the Queen visited Ireland in 1849 and then not again for fifty years. Jeremiah continued to offer '. . . Crosses Brooches Necklets Earrings Scarf Pins Celtic, Gold and Silver Connemara Marble and Irish Spar Jewellery' as late as 1892. The contemporary firm of E.M. Goggin & Co of 20 Nassau Street also advertised '. . . Irish Spar and Marble Jewellery Crystal and Amethyst Stone Goods in gold and silver mounts &c'. Waterhouse & Co were the other important 'wholesale working jewellers' in this field. Identifiable pieces of early Connemara marble jewellery and other Irish semi-precious stones are surprisingly rare, but the annular and penannular Celtic brooches are quite common. They can be mistaken for contemporary Scottish work, from which they are sometimes distinguishable by a certain fineness of detail, as well as from the original advertisements. Craftsmen in both counties drew extensively on the designs of Celtic metalwork in public collections. The author possesses a silver brooch identical with one displayed by Waterhouse's at the Great Exhibition but marked on the reverse 'Made in Scotland'. Unlike some of the Irish examples, which usually have a safety catch on the widest part of the ring, it is fastened, as was the original, by moving the pin. Presumably, the more secure modern fastening of pieces such as the Tara brooch replicas was thought desirable in view of their cost. Some of the alleged replicas are not in fact made by the same techniques, for example all the decoration may be cast where the original was chased, beaten, or had wires added. In addition, details may differ radically; the knobbed thistle brooch shown at the Great Exhibition (see p 72) appears in the illustration to have granular work on the knobs while the original has an incised diamond interlace. Such replicas were made usually of silver or gold but subsequently, aided by the Art Nouveau movement, the Celtic revival designs appear in less precious materials until today when plastic in its various forms, and very poor castings, are virtually supreme.

The Claddagh ring

The origin of the Claddagh ring, the design of which shows a crowned heart held by two hands, is obscure. It clearly has affinities with the three-part gimmel ring in which the hands move to conceal linked hearts but it would seem that the design genuinely had a long association with the fishing community of the Claddagh, just outside the walls of Galway. The already long-established firm of Dillon's of Galway revived the design in the mid-nineteenth century and it is stated that it was the only ring made in Ireland ever worn by Queen Victoria. Examples have been given to other important visitors, such as Queen Alexandra and King Edward VII, and taken as gifts to distant shores. It has retained its popularity as a masculine ornament and as a token between friends, the significance of the design being interpreted as 'Let love and friendship reign'. The Claddagh ring is quite commonly met with and may be difficult to date since TD, for Thomas Dillon, has appeared continuously on Galway examples.

JEWELLERY OF SENTIMENT

Brooches and rings

Jewellery of sentiment has always been made for holidaymakers, being exchanged between them as well as taken home. Christian names and pet names, tokens of affection and friendship and symbols of good luck proliferate on inexpensive ornaments, particularly brooches and rings. The more usual emblems of friendship include linked hands, buckle rings (exchanged between schoolgirls up to the 1950s) and the cabalistic word *Mizpah* (Genesis xxxi, 49: The Lord watch between me and thee, when we are absent one from another.). Old symbols have frequently been revived and reinterpreted. The crowned, clasped hands of the Claddagh ring were advertised in 1900 as meaning 'Love and friendship reign' by 'T. Dillon, Irish Art Jeweller of Galway and Athlone', and the linked hearts of the traditional Scottish luckenbooth brooches might be diminished to a trivial offering between acquaintances. Three-part gold gimmel or fede rings, in which twin hearts were masked by clasped hands and revealed only to those who knew the secret, were popular in the early 1900s, as were motto rings with letters deeply incised in a plain gold band. A more costly version of these was that in which the message was spelt out by the initial letters of the stones set in the band.

The usual British good luck symbols are a black cat, a four-leaved clover, a horseshoe – open end upwards 'so the luck does not run out', a sprig of white heather and a wishbone. They may occur singly or in combination with each other, with personal names, names of localities or local emblems. The four-leaved clover may become the three-leaved shamrock, traditionally Irish but, like the Scottish white heather, a universal British charm by late Victorian times. Because of its Christmas association, the wishbone's luck may be reinforced by a spray of mistletoe. In the 1920s, the black cat appears in enamel (tailless in the Isle of Man, so that it becomes a local item still sold and given away in hundreds each season), and is subsequently metamorphosed into the walking cat of the Felix cartoon.

Dating jewellery of sentiment is very difficult, since in its souvenir context it stands outside fashion and may continue to be sold long after the firm that made it has gone out of business. The earlier pieces, which seldom antedate the Great Exhibition, are well made with good quality fastenings. They are often in silver, with the surface enriched with weak and irrelevant floral ornament, but low carat gold also was used. The colour contrasts found in fashionable jewellery filtered down to the souvenir trade and a trivial floral motto brooch, selling in the 1890s at 1s 6d, may show as many as five different alloys and textured finishes. By the end of the century the brooches had become more flimsy, liable to damage merely from the pressure needed to fasten their poorer pins and difficult to keep in good condition. Die stamping was usual, as with most mass-produced Victorian jewellery, and the cheapness of the holidaymakers' ephemeral tokens is often betrayed by small size as well as lack of substance. Floral motto and *Mizpah* bar brooches are seldom more than 1½in long while the roughly oval luck emblems are about 1in overall.

As methods of making durable imitation brilliants improved, and their cost declined, they became commoner in the cheapest pieces. At first, only the lucky clover glittered, while the motto, town name or localising symbol was carried out in plain metal. Between the wars, small imitation stones were commonly pavé-set in solid backgrounds in all-over designs. After the end of World War 1 the influence of Art Nouveau reached the souvenir shops. Since the same firms made costume as well as souvenir jewellery, small silver and enamel brooches in curvilinear designs, or depicting the fashionable dragonflies or lizards (the latter remained favourites until the 1940s), appear on the same display cards as those with combinations of wishbones, horseshoes, and local emblems. 'Bluebirds of happiness', gulls, anchors, and later arrows, sun rays and other Art Deco forms, were also made, in Birmingham, London and on the continent. Towards the end of the period under consideration, cheap enamel items were usually on base metal but both Art Nouveau and Art Deco types persist.

After about 1890, mother-of-pearl became popular as a background for symbols of sentiment or local emblems. When the motif is of solid silver, firmly attached to its ground, and the pin is well made, the piece is likely to be early. The formidable hatpins required to secure Edwardian hats might be provided with heads fashioned from substantial discs of pearl shell set with imitation stones; examples may be seen in the Manx Museum, Douglas. The markings on the cards from which they were sold suggest that more brilliantly irridescent pearl shell souvenir brooches of the 1920s and 1930s were made abroad, most probably in the Far East. Their motifs, often enamelled, are roughly wired to their bases. The same wires help to attach the mount to the tiepin-style bar fastening, which has usually rusted. Worked pearl shell items, for example shrimps stained pink, were also imported. Since the 1950s, pearly plastic has been used as a background, particularly for hideous heart-shaped name brooches. Some genuine carved pearl ornaments still trickle in, notably from Taiwan, but these are folk craft gifts, not localised souvenirs.

Charms

Charms for watch chain and bracelet have an enduring popularity. Despite the murmurings of those irritated by its rattle, the bracelet has endured from at least Georgian times. The range of symbols is extensive. Lucky beans and pigs jostle various sun symbols such as the swastika, whose attraction was destroyed by political associations. The diversity is enormous, from padlocks and hearts or local emblems and coats of arms to any diminutive item that an ingenious craftsman can contrive: Shetland sweaters stretched on their drying frames, a model of Shakespeare's birthplace or an intricately jointed flexible fish. Exotic pieces often creep on to the charm tray – scraps of abalone shell, tiki figures, hearts and ferns of New Zealand jadeite. Foreign charms were, and are, imported wholesale. In the 1920s and 1930s, a Douglas shop offered Italian crescents, crosses and axe symbols carved from mother-of-pearl. The last, like the coral sprigs sold with them, have an apotropaic significance, the supposed power to ward off evil influences, reaching back to ancient Troy. More recently, equally ancient symbols such as the Egyptian looped ankh cross have reappeared.

METAL-PLATED NATURAL OBJECTS

In 1840 and 1843, the Birmingham firm of Elkington's was granted patents (Nos 8447 & 9807) for a process by which natural objects such as acorns, grouse claws or leaves could be electroplated or electrotyped. Elaborate pieces based on the *Victoria regia* waterlily were shown at the Great Exhibition. Leafwork became a fashionable hobby, patronised by Prince Albert, and both Elkington's and Palmer's of Newgate Street, London sold kits for amateur use. This made possible the production of personal souvenirs but it seems that it was not until the 1950s that the process became popular with the makers of craft souvenirs. Now, natural objects such as Stratford-on-Avon's leaves from the Forest of Arden, or the ubiquitous sea horse, abound. Because of the high cost of metal, copper or silver are used in preference to gold, with which leaves from the Hesperides are plated for sale in the Canary Islands.

PERSONAL ORNAMENTS

A wide range of personal ornaments has been localised as souvenirs.

Silver (*left*) and gilt (*right*) engraved cufflinks bearing the three-legs emblem of the Isle of Man, both mounted on West's patent clips and showing badly centred motif. Thin metal and poor quality workmanship suggest a late Victorian date.

Their types reflect changing fashions, and a knowledge of the history of dress may help to suggest dates. Thus cravat pins are followed by tie pins, fleetingly revived by the 1960s fad for cravat-like neckwear, and are then succeeded by the neat modern tie tack. Similarly, the size of brooches partly reflects current modes. Inexpensive souvenir ornaments, like jewellery of sentiment, are normally stamped (later cast) and were mass-produced mainly in the Midlands of England. The cufflinks illustrated here are unusual in being engraved and may be the product of a local jeweller using patent clips as a base.

SCOTTISH JEWELLERY

As with Irish jewellery, much produced for the Scottish souvenir trade used Scottish raw materials or traditionally Scottish motifs such as the crowned hearts of the luckenbooth brooch or the thistle, or revived still older designs. The largest category, and that with the longest continuous history, is and remains the decorated accessories of Highland dress. These enjoyed their first revival when George IV appeared in Highland dress in Edinburgh in 1822. Queen Victoria's passion for all things Scottish and the vogue for Scott's Waverley novels ensured continued popularity. The commoner items include brooches for plaids, long pins for kilts, buttons for dress jackets and mounts for sporran, skean dhu and snuffbox. Plaid brooches are often circular and the design may be more or less the revival of a Celtic pattern, including fascimiles of more notable archaeological finds, or heavily encrusted with semi-precious stones. Silver is the usual metal. Semi-precious stones include cairngorm, amethyst, topaz, garnet, carnelian and agate, all frequently claimed to be of Scottish origin. However, many of the last two seem to have been imported from the Rhine valley. This applies equally to the better quality products; the author has seen a set of accessories presented by Queen Victoria to a ghillie in which the agates are certainly of German origin. The kilt pins are usually long; in the twentieth century a thistle with the flower head fashioned from amethyst, topaz or cairngorm is common. Most of the other items are similar in style; silver, encrusted with stones, and revived Celtic designs predominate. Badges showing the motto and flower or animal symbol allegedly associated with various clans are also popular. Recently, these seem to be found only in a technically poor style of cast metal, although good quality ornaments survive otherwise.

Scotland's abundant semi-precious stones have long been exploited and seem to have been offered to travellers in the eighteenth century, both mounted and as geological specimens. Sir George Head's description of Iona children offering pebbles of the distinctive light green marble has already been quoted. This stone, which is found also on Tiree beaches, is still worked and widely sold in Scottish craft shops. The silver-mounted screw earrings illustrated were purchased on Tiree in 1960 and are examples of the dateless styles of mount which are common. Side by side with the more obviously souvenir jewellery, Scottish jewellers sold, and sell, necklaces, bracelets and brooches of oval stones mounted in slight silver settings, or bordered with seed pearls. The latter might be Scottish river pearls. In the nineteenth century, the translucent stones such as amethyst, cairngorm, garnet and topaz were fashionable but tumble-polished opaque stones have gained recent popularity. Elsewhere, the vogue for geological jewellery declined about 1910, but in Scotland the quality of the raw materials available and the skill of a few men like the Killin postmaster, Henry Horwood, ensured continuity. From about 1883 to 1930, this native of Somerset always had for sale a few brooches fashioned from local stones.

The revival of Celtic designs which influenced the work of Irish jewellers, particularly after the Great Exhibition of 1851, was evident also in Scotland. Indeed, it started there earlier. Replicas of notable archaeological finds were made and the interlacing patterns of stone carving and illuminated manuscripts were also translated into silver. Designers in the Art Nouveau style carried the fashion for Celtic interlacing patterns well into the twentieth century. Simple silver and enamel brooches were made into the 1930s and may often be found on jewellers' 'nothing over . . . ' trays although they are beginning to find favour with collectors. Those with Liberty's *Cymric* marks have already been priced out of reach of the casual buyer.

Of the Scottish jewellery illustrated, 'Iona', in which the flowing flower pattern surrounds a cruciform void as an allusion to the holy isle, is fairly typical of evolved Art Nouveau although this piece, like the small oval enamel brooch, is probably post-1918. The silver penannular brooch is likely to be of a similar date and seems to have been copied from one shown at the Great Exhibition by Waterhouse of Dublin but is clearly marked 'Made in Scotland'. A brooch differing only in the detail of the design on the head of the pin was still offered in silver, silver gilt or gold in 1973 by A. Barrie & Son of Edinburgh. They suggest that 'the intriguing Celtic interwoven design' typifies 'everlasting friendship' and that possession of the brooch 'is to recapture in some measure at least, the flavour of the glamour and romance of far-off times'. The brooch of heather stems mounted in stag's horn is described in more detail in chapter 2.

Silver luckenbooth brooches from Scotland: nineteenth century (*centre*), others earlier and cast, not stamped.

Luckenbooth brooches

Luckenbooth brooches, their name deriving from the locked booths of the Edinburgh silversmiths, seem to have originated as fairings exchanged as tokens of affection. Their design of a crowned heart or hearts is clearly related to that of the Claddagh ring. Traditionally, the brooches were made in silver (or silvered base metals) but gold examples were produced in the nineteenth century and semi-precious stones may also have been added, particularly in the twentieth century. These may form thistle blooms, a development of the design shown on the right of the illustration. Unless they were very large and made during the brief periods when silver jewellery had to be hallmarked, luckenbooth brooches are hard to date. Early pieces are likely to be cast, while those of Victorian date are frequently stamped and have their surfaces enriched with weak patterns according to contemporary taste. This tyle survived into the Edwardian period. Later twentieth century examples tend to be wiry and polished to a high gloss.

6 Ceramics

Ceramic souvenirs have a long history. In the period under consideration, virtually every innovation in fabric and method of decoration was ultimately applied to produce items for the souvenir trade. In general, souvenir production was a sideline for the larger British firms, with the notable exception of Goss, but on the continent there seems to have been a number of factories which made little else. Since imports of souvenir ceramics were not listed separately, it is almost impossible to decide how much of the trade was in the hands of manufacturers outside the British Isles. It has been the English items, again such as those made by Goss, that have in the main attracted collectors. Thus it is hard to judge on the basis of pieces currently on the market how big a share of the original sales was that of the English potters but it would seem that at least two-thirds of the ceramic souvenirs from 1870–1914 and 1920–30 must have been imported.

To some extent, ceramic souvenirs can be divided into classes even though their production was spread over a number of factories. In table wares there are transfer-printed cream-coloured earthenware, later transfer-printed topographical view wares (notably pink ware), photographic view wares, a variety of painted wares, and china and earthenware relief moulded wares. In most categories, firms copied each others' successful lines and techniques. There was considerable pirating and, particularly with transfer-printed ceramics bearing topographical views, designs originally found in one medium, such as engraved illustrations in guide books, would appear in another. A great deal remains to be discovered about the production of souvenir

Plate 16 Traditional ceramic souvenirs: (1) Pink ware mug with relief gilt edelweiss, 'A present from Newcastle on Tyne' German, (2) Teapot with coloured view of Castletown, Isle of Man, by P. Donath, Silesia (marked S below coronet), (3) Early transfer-printed mug, view of Douglas in red, hand-coloured flowers, (4) Modern miniatures: view dish, Ramsey; Tower Bridge mug, (5) Pink ware mug, 'A present from Douglas', (6) Cup and saucer, 'A present from the Isle of Man', 1930s, possibly eastern, (7) Miniature Belleek jug, 1950s.

ceramics since it is usually beneath the notice of serious students of applied arts, and two wars and other upheavals have obliterated the records of factories, wholesalers and retailers. Categories are described here with as much information as possible, and some more or less informed conjectures.

Goss

Goss is often thought of as being synonymous with souvenir china and it is forgotten that the firm, established by William Henry Goss at Stoke-on-Trent about 1858, initially specialised in fine porcelain, high-quality terracotta and parian, and with jewelled wares vying with those produced at Minton or Worcester. Floral jewellery also was an important part of the pottery's output, a form of ornament which is still made by several firms as gift ware. With the help of his oldest son, Adolphus W.H. Goss, the founder evolved a range of china which was destined to become one of the most successful types of souvenir ever to be marketed. Basically, this consisted of small ornamental pieces, made in the firm's ivory porcelain and decorated with coats of arms. Both father and son had antiquarian leanings and the shapes of many of the items were copied from early vessels preserved in museums throughout the British Isles. The coats of arms were painted in a range of colours developed by Goss senior. Allegedly, Goss souvenirs were produced for every town in the United Kingdom that had a coat of arms.

These simple and inexpensive ornaments proved so popular that by the end of the century there were over 500 stockists. Normally, there was only one agent in a town and initially only its arms would appear on models of its local antiquities. In 1900, J.J. Jarvis of Enfield, Middlesex, realised the interest which had developed in the ware and issued a duplicated list of authorised agents, together with details of the shapes and arms available. Before long, this *Goss Record* became the bible of the League of Goss Collectors for which the firm annually produced a special model, such as a copy of one of the vases found by Sir Arthur Evans at Knossos in Crete and preserved in the Ashmolean Museum at Oxford. After William Henry Goss died in 1906, his younger sons Victor Henry and William Huntley carried on the business. Despite the early death of the former in a riding accident in 1913 the firm survived the war.

The League of Goss Collectors was transformed in 1918 into the International League of Goss Collectors, which published a new edition of the *Goss Record* and still had its special models. Members could exchange duplicate models, take part in competitions and obtain at reduced prices books relating to their twin interests in heraldry and porcelain.

As with other really successful categories of souvenirs, the armorial china spread and holidaymakers on day trips to Cherbourg or Boulogne could find Goss china alongside the equally popular and familiar Mauchline ware. As will be seen later, it was also subject to the sincerest form of flattery. In addition to the special historical shapes, a wide range or more or less useful table ware and toilet table accessories were produced, together with ornaments, in all over thirty different small vases and more elaborate items. The historical pieces were described in some detail on their bases – usually the class of object, its date and place of finding and the collection in which it was preserved. Between 1884 and 1914, pieces bear numbers indicating the year in which the shape was registered. As the range increased, any arms could be ordered on any shape but only the single agent for a particular locality could supply its arms on its peculiar antiquities, whence the need for the exchange services of the International League. The more elaborate items bear the firm's punning rebus, a further reflection of the Goss passion for heraldry, of a gos(s)hawk ducally gorged. The 1930s saw a decline in the firm's fortunes and since it now produced no alternative ranges it closed during World War II. The models, blocks, etc are now the property of Messrs Ridgway & Adderley but although they have owned them since 1954 they have not attempted to revive the range.

Goss was produced in enormous quantities and has always been popular with collectors. Most of the standard items are still quite common and should be relatively inexpensive, but the more elaborate pieces such as night light holder models of Shakespeare's Cottage or Yorick's skull 'from the grave-digging scene in Hamlet' are becoming scarce and consequently overpriced. In addition to the *Goss*

Plate 17 Armorial china: (1) Goss: 'Model of incendiary bomb dropped at Maldon 16 April 1915 from a German zeppelin', height 6·3cm, *City of Salisbury*, (2) Goss: three-handled cup, height 3·7cm, *City of Winchester*, arms of city, see, and college, (3) Carlton China: Punch & Judy, 'W & R Stoke on Trent', 'Registration applied for', height 13cm, *Douglas*, (4) Arcadian China: three-handled model of 'loving cup originated by Henry of Navarre, King of France', height 4cm, arms of *England, Cumberland,* and *Whitehaven*, (5) Candlestick, probably German, diameter 8·5cm, *Scarborough*, (6) Pot, probably German, height 3·5cm, *Bournemouth*, (7) Camera, possibly Conta & Boehme, '5182', height 7cm, *Douglas*, (8) Gemma: cheese dish, marked 3/-, width 7·5cm, *Blackpool*, (9) Gemma: mug, height 3·1cm, *Portobello*, (10) Gemma: coalscuttle, height 5·2cm, *Hull*, (11) Mornesford China: fish with glass eyes, post-1920, height 7cm, *Port St Mary*, (12) Goss: 'Model of an antique pipe found among the debris of Pope's house at Twickenham', 'Rd no 622408', 12cm overall, *Portsmouth*, (13) Carlton China: two-handled mug, height 4·8cm, *Birmingham* and *Warwick*, (14) Grafton China: octagonal canister, height 5cm, two coats of arms, (15) Two-handled cup, probably German, height 3·8cm, *Barmouth*,

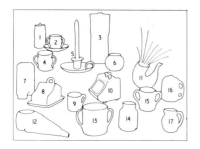

(16) Grafton China: 'Model of medieval pilgrim's bottle found at Collingbourne'. '181', 'E.F. Trenear', height 5·5cm, *Isles of Scilly*, (17) Arcadian China: jug, height 4cm, marked 'A & S Stoke on Trent' round globe with mantling above, *Rhyl*.

Record, the armorial china has acquired a considerable bibliography. There is now (1974) again a collector's magazine and postal auctions are held. 'William Henry Goss and Goss Heraldic China' (No 4 1971 *Journal of Ceramic History*) by Norman Emery gives a reasonably comprehensive list of shapes. However, it appears that the *Goss Record*, or perhaps the factory, garbled some of the place names and it may require specialised local knowledge to disentangle the actual origin of the ancient vessel modelled. However, it should not therefore be assumed that if a piece marked Goss is not listed it was not made by the firm. It may merely have evaded the compiler's attention.

Other makers of armorial souvenirs

Goss was far too successful to retain his monopoly of small armorial souvenirs for long and there was soon a host of imitators both in England and on the continent. Among the more prolific and consequently common English ranges of a similar type were the Arcadian china of A & S (Arkinstall & Sons, 1904–24, Stoke-on-Trent), Grafton China of A.B. Jones & Sons, and Carlton china of W & R (Wittshaw, Robinson & Son, 1925, Stoke-on-Trent). These are normally marked with black transfers on the base, giving the name of the range and the maker. There is also a painted code of letters and numerals. The ware is very thin, translucent and often faintly creamy in colour rather than dead white. The arms, supporters, mottos, etc are painted in brilliant but sometimes fugitive colours and the general style is reminiscent of that of later Goss products.

Plate 18   A Goss special souvenir: the Ballafletcher Fairy Cup with the arms of Peel, Isle of Man.

The imitations extend even to the same detailed copying of archaeological finds, and a similar system of licensed agents was used; for example, a Grafton china 'Model of a medieval pilgrim's bottle found at Collingbourne' with the arms of 'T. Algernon Dorrien Smith Lord Proprietor of the Isles of Scilly' and countermarked with the name of the seller, E.F. Trenear. As far as the author can discover, there was no post-1945 production of miniature armorial china but larger dishes, plates, cups, saucers, etc seem to be reappearing in increasing numbers. Maybe Goss will yet be revived.

Unmarked armorial wares are equally abundant. These generally have a more opaque, whiter body and frequently the glaze does not extend appreciably over the base. The finish may be poor, with, distorted transfers or obtrusive mould marks. It is likely that the bulk of these unmarked pieces were made on the continent. Among the marked pieces mainly of German origin are those with transfers on their bases reading Gemma (diagonally on a shield beneath a seven-pointed coronet – used by a Bohemian firm later in Czechoslovakia) and Royal Coburg. Unfortunately, the upheaval of two world wars and the subsequent partition of Germany have effectively ensured that no exhaustive list of firms exporting souvenir wares to Britain can be compiled.

BELLEEK

The Belleek pottery, established in 1857 on an islet in the river Erne in Co Fermanagh, was not initially intended to produce items for the souvenir trade. The founders, Robert William Armstrong and his

Plate 19 The Ballafletcher Fairy Cup: original in the Manx Museum.

backer, David M'Birney, co-owner of a large Dublin store, apparently hoped to undersell the English potteries in the North American market. With water power from the river for grinding, good supplies of fuel and large deposits of good china clay and exceptionally pure felspar available on John Caldwell Bloomfield's nearby Castle Caldwell estate they were well placed for the manufacture of fine porcelain. The factory soon developed a very white body that was so handled that shrinkage produced a ware of great thinness. This in part explains the unusual lightness characteristic of classic Belleek. To this body was applied a novel glaze developed by Jules Joseph Henri Brianchon. To produce it, ten parts of a salt such as bismuth nitrate were stirred into thirty parts of melted resin, followed by forty-five parts oil of lavender. When this mixture was cool, a further fifty parts of lavender oil were added. The resultant finish, when fired, reproduced the nacreous irridescent lustre of a pearl shell. Its tone could be varied by using a different salt. The British patent (No 1896 of 1857) was issued on 1 January 1858 but the inventor also licensed the use of his glaze elsewhere in Europe. When the British patent expired on 1 January 1872 other firms took to producing wares closely resembling Belleek in technique.

At first, the firm concentrated on luxury items including elaborate Parian statuary and ornamental pieces, in which unglazed Parian was contrasted with the glassy sheen of Brianchon's glaze. Typically, these included marine life – coral, shells, mermaids, sea horses, sea urchins – or floral elements. Baskets of flowers were particularly highly valued by the Victorians. Early designs were registered. When the two founders died in 1884, their successors sold the business to a group of local men; Armstrong's sons emigrated to North America and continued to produce ware of Belleek type at the Trenton Pottery, New Jersey. After 1884, the original pottery produced pieces requiring less exacting handwork, and a more definite souvenir element appears. About 1877 the firm made a marine tea service for Queen Victoria, so its products were doubtless already thought of as typical of Ireland and taken home by the discerning visitor.

The earliest mark appears to be an impressed 'Belleek Pottery', which is found on unglazed Parian statuary. Later the firm traded as M'Berney & Armstrong, then M'Berney & Co. Their more usual trademark incorporated those epitomes of Irish souvenirs, a round tower – with a wolfhound to the left and an Irish harp to the right – and three shamrock leaves at each end of a ribbon bearing the name Belleek. After the McKinley Tariff Act of 1891 came into operation 'Ireland' also appeared in the mark. As far as is known, all pieces produced at Belleek are marked, the apparent exceptions being elaborate modelled items to which the mark, on a pad of Parian, was once attached with a spot of translucent flint glaze.

Modern Belleek still retains much of the charm of the nineteenth century pieces and some items may occasionally be passed off as early work. However, at the lower end of the price range and with the more obvious souvenir items this is unlikely to happen. A visit to any souvenir shop, particularly those maintained in the airports, will indicate the present range. Basically, it comprises small ostensibly useful items such as ashtrays, tableware and more elaborate modelled pieces in which the last vestiges of the marine style are apparent. Shamrocks in low relief, bright green or a less aggressive golden yellow, proliferate over what would normally be flat surfaces and there is a distinct aura of 'a present from Ireland'.

CERAMIC SOUVENIR MAKERS OUTSIDE THE BRITISH ISLES

There must have been innumerable factories making souvenirs in Austria, Czechoslovakia, Germany, and the Low Countries but it is extremely difficult to obtain precise information about them. Among the more notable were Conta & Boehme of Possneck in Saxony, whose factory was established about 1790. Many of their products were in fine hard porcelain, Hartporzellan, or a ware similar in appearance to Parian. The earlier, generally unmarked pieces are heavier than the later work. The factory also produced fairings such as matchboxes, miniature vases for the boudoir, and the comic 'go-to-bed' groups which, towards the end of the century, appear with a resort's coat of arms and the legend 'A present from . . .' The firm's mark was an upraised hand within a shield, usually stamped into the biscuit before firing. In view of the amount of souvenirs with this mark, one is inclined to wonder whether it was pirated along with the designs; it occurs also in relief, and transfer-printed over the glaze. Other firms known to be continental include one using the mark 'E S B' and Franz Tuhten & Co. After the Tariff Act of 1891, the country of origin is indicated.

Japanese firms entered the European souvenir market later but once they had established connections they supplied a large proportion of the cheaper ceramic souvenirs. This helped to enhance their reputation as copyists. Country of origin is sometimes indicated but regrettably often the legend merely reads 'foreign'. The extent to which the Japanese were popularly supposed to have cornered the market is illustrated by the venerable story that pottery leprechauns were sold in Ireland marked 'Made in Japan' in Irish. In the last fifteen years or so souvenirs of eastern origin have again appeared.

CRAFT POTTERIES

Apart from the period 1939–45, interest in the art of the potter has been steadily increasing since the 1920s. Thus potteries depending largely on seasonal sales to passing tourists are becoming a feature of resort areas. Plate 21 shows a random selection of their products from the author's collection. Such potteries may be split into four groups, the first of which comprises those run by great potters practising their craft, here represented by the shepherd's purse dish and small stoneware vase by the younger Leach, purchased in Stratford-on-Avon. These are few in number and seldom outlive their founders.

There are also a few potteries, our second group, which once supplied the domestic needs of their area and had a thriving export trade – represented here by a small bowl from the Branham pottery, Barnstaple – but are now somewhat anachronistic survivors. Since a pottery can be set up relatively cheaply and can be viable with a small staff while yielding a readily saleable product, it is a minor industry favoured by those trying to foster employment in areas losing their populations. Thus CoSIRA and the Highlands and Islands Development Board include potters in their lists of rural craftsmen.

The third group is made up of a few producers of hand potted wares who have created so good a sales organisation that their wares are available throughout holidaymakers' Britain. Some, such as the distinctive black wares of Prinknash, are plain and take their place among the craft souvenirs. Others, like the localised jugs of Devonmoor, are more blatantly tourist-orientated but still useful and attractive. Unfortunately, a few people have realised that quality is not vital to sales. Thus moulded pieces and decorated 'bought-in' wares may be used to gull the public, who may well believe that they are buying hand-thrown wares. The final deterioration, the fourth group, is the cast gnome or cottage produced with the aid of a bought mould. The number of 'lucky' pixies in the British Isles is beyond belief. It is no longer so easy to view these many aids to parting people and money collected together, since Dr Gerald Gardener's Witches Mill collection has been exported from the Isle of Man to the USA.

FIGURES

A lastingly popular type of souvenir was the ornamental figure, or figure group, which evolved from the traditional fairing and mantelpiece ornaments. In the period under consideration a major producer seems to have been Conta & Boehme of Possneck in Saxony, although other continental firms and, later, Japanese producers also catered for the British market. W.S. Bristowe gives a comprehensive account of the known types in his *Victorian China Fairings* but intentionally omits the more obviously souvenir pieces. He indicates that serial numbers as high as 4,000 on the Conta & Boehme pieces belong to souvenirs. These seldom seem to carry the firm's usual mark, a bent arm with dagger, like that used by Springer & Co, Elbogen. It is probable that plaques with numbers in the hundreds were made by the former.

Boxes were made by the same firms, even from the same moulds, although this might make them so top heavy as to be useless as containers, for example Laxey Wheel, with a half inch box below a seven inch model of the well-known Manx water wheel. During the period 1919–39, the armorial china firms issued figures. Hewitt and Leadbetter (Willow Art) produced a model of a three-legged dog, Prince Toby Orry, to order for a Douglas firm, using a contemporary postcard as a pattern. Similarly, a German factory's Ladies of Llangollen was designed after a postcard. It seems that F. & S. Salaman of 136 Fenchurch Street, London transmitted ideas and orders from English shops to Conta & Boehme but, as has been indicated, Manx firms appear to have dealt directly with Germany, their 'Hi, Kelly' figures

Plate 20 Three-legged teapots: Staffordshire majolica, probably Cobridge Works (*left*), later Thuringian copy with 'Chelsea' anchor mark (*right*).

being ordered from a firm called Greiner's (phonetic spelling).

FIGURE TEAPOTS

Teapots in the form of x's cottage are fairly common although the majority are post-1920. One other seemingly unique group of figure pots is worthy of further description. These are the Staffordshire majolica three-legged men sold in the Isle of Man. On the evidence of glaze and fabric, they seem likely to have been produced by Brownfield's Cobridge works. Some bear an indication that they were made for Broughton's of Douglas. There are three basic types: a sailor seated on a coil of rope carrying an ensign, which is fairly common, a rarer sailor holding the rope's end to make a handle, and a man astride a branch. The last is very rare. The example in the Manx Museum is a later Thuringian copy bearing Chelsea's red anchor mark.

LITHOPHANES

Lithophanes, or 'shadowed drawings', used an ingenious method of moulding a hard porcelain so that when a light was placed behind it a picture, drawn in the varying translucency of different thicknesses of porcelain, was revealed. The first British patent was granted in 1827 and there were licensed producers in France, Germany and Holland. It is not known when the lithophane was taken up on a large scale by souvenir manufacturers but it is unlikely to have been before the patents expired. Items which enjoyed a large and concentrated sale, such as the pairs of plaques showing Edward VII and his queen, are likely to have been made according to the traditional method, as were the luxury lithophanes made by Belleek, Copeland, Goss and Wedgwood. However, it is difficult to believe that so involved a process would not have been modified when used to make mass souvenirs. It is possible in fact that all lithophanic souvenirs, such as a set of coffee cups painted with the characteristic blue 'windmills and flowers' of modern Delft but revealing a picture of Douglas Bay, Isle of Man in

their bases when held to the light, were of twentieth century continental or even eastern manufacture. The existence of a miniature
three-handled crested mug with Manx arms and a lithophane portrait
of Edward VII in the base lends credence to this dating.

PARIAN AND RELATED VITRIFIED BISCUIT PORCELAIN

Parian is a highly vitrified biscuit porcelain originally developed by
Copeland & Garrett for the production of statuary. At first, impurities
in the main ingredient, felspar, gave a yellowish hue but later bodies
utilising purer felspar have the crystalline whiteness associated with
the fine marble of Paros, from which the name derives. During the
1840s a modified Parian, made from sixty-seven parts felspar to thirty-
three parts china clay, was produced. This was used at first for fine
tableware, luxury ornaments and jewellery but later in the nineteenth
century it slipped down the scale to become a vehicle for the souvenir
manufacturers. Even before the expiration of the original patents,
other firms produced similar fabrics. The first English souvenirs were
mainly in the Parian's original line of statuary, such as busts of Shakespeare, but when continental firms entered the market the range produced was much larger.

The body lent itself to moulding, and figures, or vases incorporated
in figure groups, were common. Both traditional Germanic models
and more clearly localised pieces were made. Thus for the Isle of Man
there was a range of three-legged figures, an allusion to the insular
arms, in tinted biscuit porcelain. Sometimes these merely stand
against the support of the vase bud otherwise they perform some
action intended to bring out the humour of their tri-pedal state, such
as climbing a style. Similar figures also occur in the coloured and gilt
glazed ware typical of German fairings.

A particularly attractive form of souvenir to modern eyes, is the
relief plaque in which the design in white is presented against a tinted
monochrome ground. The choice of ground colour, soft green, blue
or purplish rose, suggests that the influence of Wedgwood's jasper

plaques was at work. According to Sir Arthur Church, the jasper body was made of fifty-nine parts sulphate of barium, twenty-nine parts clay, ten parts ground flint and two parts carbonate of barium and it was inclined to be temperamental when fired. Since these larger German plaques were mass produced it would seem that they owe only their colour schemes to jasper. Indeed, they may be made by a different technique, the design and the background seemingly moulded together rather than being fashioned separately. Architectural subjects are common, such as Ann Hathaway's cottage or the great Laxey Wheel. Rectangular moulded picture frame shapes are more plentiful than the round type lacking moulded edges. Apart from range numbers scratched in the surface of the back they are unmarked, but are certainly German and presumably from the same prolific factories as other ranges of ceramic souvenirs.

RIBBON AND OTHER WALL PLATES

From about 1880, souvenir plates with pierced rims, through which coloured ribbon could be threaded to enhance their decorative effect, were imported. British potteries produced such plates with elaborately painted centres but all examples localised by view or legend seem to be foreign. Ribbon plates were traditional ornaments on 'narrow boats', presumably because they could readily be hung on the wall and thus were unlikely to be broken and did not take up valuable shelf space in the tiny cabins. Similar considerations may have helped to make them popular in the cramped back-to-backs of the industrial towns. They occur both in porcelain and china, thickly glazed to hide the edges of the punched out pattern, with all the variations of German-made topographical views. Star and other fancy piercings apparently date from after 1900.

White plates with scanty overglaze floral designs incorporating tiger lilies, roses, lilies of the valley – with one blue-green and one yellow-green leaf – forget-me-nots in pale colours, and gold legends are usually Austrian. Similar wares were made in Czechoslovakia.

Most of the plates are fairly large, about 8–9in, but smaller examples, often in pairs, exist. Oval plates, with two handles and holes for a suspension cord in the foot ring at the back, occur in the same Austrian floral designs and were presumably painted in the same factories. In the twentieth century, wall plates saying 'A present from . . .' were imported from China and Japan and the legend may be married to typically 'eastern for the European market' owls, storks, etc. Relief-moulded wall plates also occur and it is difficult to draw the distinction between a plate and a plaque.

SUNDERLAND PINK LUSTRE AND PINK WARE

Early in the nineteenth century the Staffordshire potters developed a metallic-appearing finish for earthenware. The tone and colour of this lustre varied according to the ingredients used, the thickness applied and the colour and nature of the body. Wedgwood's introduced the old Chinese method of mottling lustre by spraying it with thin oil, through a muslin filter, before firing. This technique was used so often by Sunderland potters, notably on the pink lustre surrounds to transfer-printed views of the Wearmouth Bridge, that mottled pink lustre is often known as Sunderland lustre. Twenty-two different views of 'the longest single-span cast-iron bridge in the world', which opened in 1796, was much altered in 1859 and replaced in 1929, are known. Eight of them are fairly common. The potteries issuing them apparently obtained their transfers from the same sources so identical scenes appear on the products of more than one pottery. It should be noted also that views showing the bridge before it was levelled and widened were still used after 1859.

The older potteries in Sunderland were founded at the end of the eighteenth century. William Maling started the Sunderland Pottery, locally known as the Garrison Pottery because it was near the Sunderland Barracks, in 1762. When he moved to Newcastle upon Tyne in 1815 it was taken over by John Phillips, once one of his works managers, and the pottery continued to function until 1867. Phillips had an interest initially in the rival Hylton Pottery, situated some three miles west of the town. This was subsequently operated by his former partner, Robert Dixon, with William Austin. Alexander Phillips, a relation of John's, joined the partnership in 1826 and when Austin left in 1840 the firm became Dixon, Phillips & Co, retaining this name until it closed in 1865. The other main Sunderland potteries were the Low Ford, or Dawson's, which was in production before 1796 and survived until 1864, Southwick, or Scott's, which worked about 1788–1899 and outlived most of its competitors by more than twenty years, and its neighbour the Wear Pottery, founded some ten years earlier, which survived until 1883.

In addition to the useful wares, mainly bowls, jugs, mugs and plates decorated with views of the bridge, these potteries made a wide variety of domestic wares and gift china. They supplied fairgrounds with prizes and itinerant hawkers with stock. Their products are often found with personal inscriptions, frequently much worn. These commemorate events such as weddings and christenings and were often added to order by retailers, who refired the piece in a low-temperature 'muffle kiln'. Production of such souvenirs seems to have been a feature of some resorts. A late nineteenth century attraction at Douglas was a craftsman who would add both inscription and pattern, in bright overglaze colours, to plain white plates. One such plate, given by a grateful lodger to his landlady's daughter, has a design of strawberries, the little girl's name and the date on which it was painted. In this way, Sunderland products could become souvenirs of other towns.

Other Sunderland specialities were the religious or nautical plaques. These usually take the form of a frame, often lustred or painted yellow to suggest gilt, surrounding a transfer-printed design or hand-painted text, and might be stark injunctions such as 'Prepare to meet thy god', or lively pictures of sailing craft, with verses with a strongly patriotic flavour. Similar pink lustre was made at Bristol, Liverpool, Newcastle upon Tyne – the town to which Maling moved – and Swansea, as well as in Staffordshire itself. Although it is impossible to establish the connecting link, it seems likely that it was the popularity of the Sunderland ware combination of pink lustre and black trans-fer-printing that led to the production of 'pink ware' by the German potteries that served the souvenir trade. Sewell & Co's St Anthony's Pottery at Newcastle upon Tyne was established in 1780 and '. . . sent to Holland and other Continental countries' the product of two or three firings a week of cream coloured ware throughout much of the nineteenth century. Nevertheless if a 'pink ware' mug, decor-ated with gilt applied relief flowers and the legend 'A present from Newcastle upon Tyne' – see plate 16 (1) – is inverted it will be found to be stamped 'Made in Germany', which perhaps explains why the flowers are modelled on edelweiss. It would seem that the English pink lustre originals could have reached the continent through the trade in cream coloured ware. William Smith of the Staf-ford Pottery, Stockton-on-Tees, was so succesful with his exports that he established a branch pottery at Genappes, near Mons in Belgium, as early as 1825. As far as can be discovered, pink ware souvenirs, whether localised by views or merely by gilt inscriptions, were never made in the British Isles although it seems improbable that some did not have inscriptions added.

Pink ware is still quite common but is becoming less so as its popu-larity with collectors of Victoriana grows. Most items are of useful shapes and sizes, with cups, mugs and plates predominating as survi-vors. Pieces of a readily portable size such as egg cups, sugar bowls and teapots may be met with but, as it was exclusively a souvenir ware, really unwieldy things like bowls and ewers are unlikely to be found. Since so many firms were involved in producing it and its popularity extended over so long a period it is not surprising that there is a very wide range of shapes. It may be that the simpler forms are early while elaborate mouldings into panels or ribs appealed to the more florid taste of the later part of Queen Victoria's reign. The range of views used is enormous and covers monuments to local pride and Victorian progress such as lunatic asylums and St Pancras Station as well as the more usual resort scenes. As with other printed souvenirs, there was a tendency for structures, particularly piers, to survive on pink ware views long after they had been altered or destroyed. Regrettably, it is impossible to discover precisely how the factories obtained their views. There is often a very close resemblance between the views on Mauchline woodware, glass paperweights and pink ware. It would therefore seem probable that English transfer makers sold, perhaps unwittingly, their designs abroad and there was clearly considerable piracy between manufacturers in various fields. The author has been given information that in the post-1918 period picture postcards would be supplied by wholesalers to continental firms as patterns, particularly when exclusive designs were being ordered. Hyman A. Abrahams & Sons of Houndsditch, London, 'Mugs, cups and saucers &c, decorated to order . . . or with views of any particular place or town', seems to have been an important middleman in England in the 1880s.

TRANSFER-PRINTED TOPOGRAPHICAL VIEWS

Origins

The Staffordshire potters included views of castles, cathedrals, country houses and watering places in the designs they used for their blue-printed pottery from about 1790 onwards. These were originally offered mainly in large sets but nevertheless must have sold partly on local patriotism – views of buildings in the United States were certainly produced for sale there. Tableware showing resort scenes – the beach at Brighton, the cliffs of Dover, Cowes Harbour, East Cowes, Whitby, Yarmouth or such obligatory 'sights' as Guy's Cliff and Kenilworth Castle, Warwickshire – was issued by Enoch Wood of Burslem. Other important potters of similar wares were W. Adams of Stoke-on-Trent (London views circa 1816 and English views), James and Ralph Clews, Ralph Hall, J.W. Riley, J. Stubbs and John and William Ridgway. The last two worked together at the Cauldon Place Pottery 1814–30. During this period they produced a fine series decorated with views of Oxford and Cambridge colleges, subjects which appeared also on papier mâché ornaments. While initially Staffordshire blue-and-white was far from being a souvenir ware, it is clear from advertisements as early as 1841 that items, particularly plates, were sold apart from the full services by itinerant dealers who purchased their stock from the potteries and then travelled from town to town setting up shop in premises rented for short periods. Presumably, when wares with local views were available, these would be selected as most likely to enjoy a ready sale. Many of these designs had a long life and in recent years scenic plates have been sold from 'antique' shops as a better-class souvenir.

CREAM-COLOURED EARTHENWARE

Transfer-printing was used from the late 1770s on cream-coloured earthenware, notably by Sadler & Green of Liverpool (on Wedgwood's products) and the Leeds Pottery. The colours most often found are various blacks and reds. From the beginning of its popularity, cream-coloured earthenware was offered with personal crests, etc. It is therefore not surprising that a souvenir ware evolved alongside special products for friendly societies and such durable designs as the 'Farmers' Arms'. Contemporary engravings were freely adapted. Comparison of designs makes it clear that despite the protection of the Registration of Designs Act of 1842, engravers of views for use on pots drew on those used in guide books or by their rivals. Piracy might be veiled by altering foreground figures and minor details: after all, the view itself was hardly copyright. In some instances, the blockmaker for guide books and topographical souvenirs may have been the same firm. Virtually identical views of the Isle of Man appear on mugs, handkerchiefs and in guide books, the signed engravings in the latter being the work of George Philip & Son of Liverpool and London.

Early souvenir topographical views in cream-coloured earthenware are printed usually on standard tableware. Rather small straight-sided mugs with a single handle, and jugs, barrel-shaped or straight-sided, are particularly common. The design is nearly always in black and the views are titled. From about 1860 onwards the magic words 'A present from . . . ' appear. There may be a little additional ornament in the form of the narrow borders common to the pottery's other products, or simple coloured lining in red, blue or green enamel. Souvenirs transfer-printed on cream wares were produced by noted as well as humble potteries. Makers of pieces sold in the Isle of Man include a number of Staffordshire firms using the services of Thomas Minton's specialist engravers, and the Liverpool Herculaneum Pottery 1793–1841.

Later English developments – Doulton

Later, Doulton seems to have been particularly fond of issuing wares which sold on patriotism. The author has seen part of a bedroom set called *Mona* with guide book views printed in brown. So bulky an item could hardly have been intended primarily as a souvenir but presumably would appeal to landladies equipping themselves for the season. Similarly, close study of a tall Art Deco coffeepot, with decoration and colouring very much in the style of their Dutch or Olde Curiosity Shoppe series, reveals that the castle depicted is Castle Rushen, Isle of Man. A similar pot is said to have a scene of Rye. One wonders if these were attempts to cash in on two markets, with localisation being obscured to ensure more general sales.

Other late developments

As the nineteenth century passed, a liking for more gaily coloured souvenirs developed together with a variety of techniques for satisfying the demand. Colours had been added by hand from the beginnings of transfer-printing but now colour-printing was cheap enough for use on the most inexpensive wares. Mass production methods

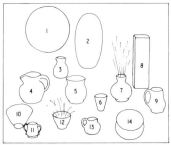

Plate 21 Modern craft pottery: (1) dish decorated with fish and weed (produced in same way as 'ferns' on Mocha ware), Dartmouth Pottery, 1950s, (2) Dish with incised design, David Leach, 1950s, (3) Stoneware vase glazed smoky blue, Durness, Scotland, 1972, (4) Jug with impressed pattern of Glastonbury Holy Thorn leaves, North Somerset Potteries, (5) Green glazed pot with sgraffito through brush strokes on neck, Brecon, 1960s, (6) White miniature pot with blue and green underglaze decoration, North Somerset Potteries, 1950s, (7) Stoneware vase, David Leach, 1950s, (8) Slab vase with abstract decoration, St Ives, 1970s, (9) Miniature mug with slip decoration, and (10) Miniature wall vase with sgraffito decoration, North Somerset Potteries, 1950s, (11) Miniature two-handled mug in lustrous black, a revival of Cistercian ware sold widely as gift ware, Prinknash Abbey, Gloucestershire, (12) Miniature pot purpose-made for flower arrangement on small scale, Angela Gibson, Stow-on-the-Wold, Gloucestershire, 1960s, (13) Squat green glazed miniature jug, Truro Potteries, (14) Round yellow pot from long-established Branham Pottery, Barnstaple, Devon, 1940s.

and low wages made it possible for overseas potteries to flood the market with brightly-painted cups, plates and ornaments. Attempts to brighten topographical items included the colouring of the ground. Sometimes this shades from blue to pink (to suggest a blue sea under a sunset sky?) or primrose yellow, dull green and rose. The former is common on small ornaments imported from Europe, particularly sets of vases. The latter is often the background on grossly over-decorated lumpish pieces of surpassing ugliness of shape. The adjuncts to the toilet table include such things as watch stands, jewel boxes – with eminently droppable handle-less lids – and pin trays, en suite, with a riot of cabbage roses, and much gilt, amid which lurks the resort's arms. These were certainly mainly German but Stafford-shire was not guiltless. After about 1890, the views may have been produced from a photographic original. Ridgway produced practical items, such as tableware including large pieces like cheese dishes, in a curious varnish brown with abundant gilding, but on the whole the photographic view wares are brightly coloured. Unlike the more austere products of the nineteenth century, they are still quite common.

WARES PERSONALISED OR LOCALISED ONLY BY INSCRIPTION

Virtually all eighteenth and nineteenth century potteries would take commissions for commemorative pieces for christenings, weddings and the like. Lowestoft seems to have made a speciality of these and, as has been indicated, they also occur in lustre. Such pieces would normally be decorated in the same style as the rest of the pottery's products. It is therefore not surprising that localising inscriptions, which make the item a souvenir of a place rather than an occasion, soon appear. Thus there are many mugs dating from 1860–70 with typical contemporary designs, for example floral or birds and their nests painted in bright overglaze enamels, with 'A present from . . .' added to lure the coins from the pockets of the growing numbers of trippers. Such simple localisation remained common throughout the period under consideration.

Similar lettering might also be added by a retailer or middleman. Some German potteries seem to have exported wares with plain panels in which lettering, whether local or personal, could be added. Rather earlier Sunderland lustre was also treated in the same way. The additional inscriptions are frequently gilt and seldom durable. That this failure to withstand wear was not merely a feature of inexpensive souvenirs may be seen from the fact that the inscriptions on less than half of the surviving handsome North German punchbowls, the so-called 'Elsinore bowls', given as presents by the firm of Major Wright & Co of Elsinore to the captains of visiting vessels, can now be read in their entirety. Nevertheless, gilt inscriptions retained popularity. The adding of overglaze ornament was a pier arcade attraction in some resorts. Such work seems to have been popular both before and after World War I but has now been replaced by mass personalisation ('Your name must be here – unusual names to order') and commissions to craftsman potters.

7 Metal Souvenirs

Long before the beginning of the period under consideration, Birmingham had become the centre of the 'toy' trade. Among its early essays into souvenirs were innumerable 'Present from . . . ' snuffboxes. At the beginning of the nineteenth century, beautifully made miniature ornaments, often in precious metals, were produced for the cabinets and dolls houses of the rich. As with other fashions, there was a gradual slide down the social scale and by the end of the nineteenth century similar miniatures, particularly tiny jugs and shoes (often fitted with pincushions), were made in brass for the holiday market. Similarly, some enterprising brassfounders realised that their basic stock-in-trade of fire irons, trivets, doorknockers, etc could easily be designed to be sold as souvenirs. Thus Ann Hathaway's cottage, Dr Johnson's or Shakespeare's bust, the Lincoln imp and the Manx cat became enduring reminders of past holidays every time their unhelpful shapes were grasped to mend the fire or sweep crumbs from the cloth. Goss's idea of adding coats of arms or 'crests' was also adopted.

Pearson, Page Jewsbury Co Ltd of Witton, Birmingham, have been manufacturing such brass and copper souvenirs for well over seventy years. In their current Peerage range they have over 2,000 different types. These are localised by the addition of an enamel crest or ribbon with a placename, a small cast applied mount or a much larger (2 x 3 in) souvenir casting. Their ranges of miniature jugs, kettles, watering cans, wheelbarrows, etc are still widespread in seaside shops

Plates 22–3 Crested and emblem brassware made by Pearson, Page Jewsbury Co Ltd.

and companion sets and doorknockers also are common. There is seldom any easy aid to dating this type of brass or copper souvenir save that early twentieth century examples may contain more metal and pieces made pre-1939 may be badly tarnished as the 'needs no cleaning' finish seems then not to have been perfected. In the 1970s, a reduction in the number of outlets was found desirable as rising costs were taking the miniatures out of the minor markets for holiday trivia and only places on the overseas tourist routes, such as Bath, Stratford-on-Avon and Windsor, could yield sufficient sales to make an economic proposition.

Peerage was by no means the only name in the business and it seems likely that in the nineteenth century when small foundries were common they might make local souvenirs. Among the most handsome are the heavy trivets and kettle stands. In the Isle of Man, those with three legs were almost certainly cast by foundries such as Gelling's Mona Foundry (established 1842) while iron fender stools with the same emblem were made by local blacksmiths. Brass was also used for advertising items such as the shoe silhouettes now so avidly collected, and ash trays.

More recently, chrome metal has partly ousted brass and trivets and many crested items are abundant. Again, Birmingham is the centre with, for example, Charles Iles & Gomms Ltd holding 'dies of crests for all principal resorts in Great Britain, together with those of many towns and resorts in Great Britain'. They also make rather better quality ranges including the sterling silver charms enamelled with town crests mentioned previously.

Various processes, notably 'etching', have been used since the 1950s to produce both rather handsome topographical plaques and unbelievably tasteless wall ornaments. The latter include pseudo-negroid profiles, twee garden scenes and debased parodies of vintage cars.

With modern forge and welding equipment, metalworking has again become a practical craft for one or two men working in relatively remote areas, and thus wrought metalwork is a common feature of modern craft souvenirs, ranging from decorative pieces like candlesticks to the more substantial gates and fire baskets which can be ordered from roadside workshops. The metal-plated leaf jewellery has already been mentioned. The setting of nuts, bolts, watch parts and similar mechanical *disjecta membra* in plastic is another manifestation. Collages and patterns, sometimes abstract, sometimes representational (flowers and vintage cars are favoured subjects) are created with similar assortments of spare parts. Objet trouvé and welded scrap metal sculpture, a long way after 'The unknown political prisoner' and Bryan Kneale, are also offered rather (too?) frequently.

LAXEY SILVER

One of the unique types of souvenir sold in the Isle of Man in the late nineteenth century was cutlery marked 'Laxey Silver' between two of the island's three-legs symbols. Additional marks, also perhaps intended to deceive the ignorant into believing that they were buying solid silver, often include the initials D & A. All the pieces known are in the plainest styles and all are electroplate. Spoons and forks of various sizes are common. Indeed they are so abundant that it is clear that they were sold widely in the island to both residents and visitors. More specialised items such as sugar tongs and pickle forks are rare and are also of the same utilitarian patterns. (Tongs with the ends formed into the three-legs, often with an ingenuous lifting mechanism, were imported more recently from the continent.) No solid silver item unequivocally made from Manx metal survives. Since there was neither a major working jeweller nor hallmarking facilities in the Isle of Man it would have been manufactured and hallmarked elsewhere. Manx silver would thus be unidentifiable in the absence of an informative inscription. Since silver was quite frequently given to mine captains and similar officials such presentation pieces may well exist, but they are outside the scope of this book. The main firm manufacturing Laxey Silver was Daniel & Arter of Birmingham. They first appear in directories as 'German silver and electro spoon makers, 50 and 51, Lombard Street', in 1867. By 1879, they were also making forks and had moved to the Globe Silver Works, Highgate Street. These premises had become the Globe Nevada Silver Works by 1904 since the firm apparently specialised in cutlery on which the trade name ostensibly indicated the origin of the silver used in plating, and Nevada Silver was another equally abundant line. Daniel & Arter remained in business until 1938 (the last directory entry is 'spoon and fork manufacturers/electro plate and silversmiths' in 1934) but the misleadingly marked cutlery apparently belongs to the period 1880–1910. Considerable variations of mark exist and 'DM' or 'Manx Silver' may indicate the existence of rival manufacturers. Regrettably, no records of sales, advertisements or purchases have survived but oral tradition confirms the dates indicated.

LEAD FIGURES

The author has seen an example of an apparently unique type of souvenir, a pair of lead figures. They are three-legged and wear top hats and frock coats, like the non-sailor Manx teapot figure, but have red and white striped stockings. In this they correspond to newspaper advertisements by the Douglas firm of Witherspoon's, confectioners, 1880–1930s. The heads are made separately and nod like a nineteenth century toy. The figures can be persuaded to stand, despite the weight of the backward-kicking third leg, by adjusting a walking stick. Kept as souvenirs by a Manx family living in England, they may originally have been an advertising item, like Coupe's three-legged stick pins which were given away with tobacco, and were made possibly in a Douglas foundry. The author has also seen a composition ornamental figure of an old lady (with the normal number of legs) with a nodding head, which was reputedly a local product.

MEDALETS

Among the German-produced souvenirs of the pre-1914 period were base-metal medalets with local views and emblems or crests. Among those recorded are *Belfast*, coat of arms, spinning wheel on reverse; *Larne*, Co Antrim, coat of arms, Giant's Causeway on reverse; *Laxey Wheel*, Isle of Man, three-legs emblem on obverse. The white metal Peel Castle medallions from the same island are known to be considerably earlier and a local product. The dies survive. Similar pieces sometimes appeared among the prizes given out by amusement arcade slot machines into the 1950s. Localised medallions have been made from time to time for the jewellery trade. For example, in 1966 British Historical Medals Ltd issued a handsome sovereign-sized medalet depicting Castle Rushen and the Manx emblem. This fitted standard mounts and was a noteworthy, if short-lived, response to requests for better quality souvenirs.

SMALL METAL BOXES

The more or less useful little box has enjoyed a long life in the souvenir trade and those in metal are more durable than most. As patch boxes, they were produced in enamel in the 1780s and 90s. The designs are similar to other contemporary examples but they are localised with the words 'A trifle from . . . ' Similar little boxes with sentimental mottos were made and were doubtless sold as holiday gifts. When patches went out of fashion, the boxes became holders for cachous. The later and rather less well made examples were mass-produced in Birmingham. They may be distinguished from the eighteenth century examples more highly regarded by collectors by, among other things, the words 'A present from . . . ' and also by coloured views and crests. The presence of these indicates a date towards the end of the nineteenth century.

Snuffboxes were sold until snufftaking was superseded by cigar smoking. Ladies were offered little containers for toilet or needlework accessories. After about 1870, ornamental matchboxes became common. They usually have a roughened metal striking surface. Flat matchboxes about the size of a modern cigarette lighter were produced in very large quantities as souvenirs. The metal container often has a covering of another material, frequently 'ivorine' or a similar composition, and is localised with crests and views. After the safety match became common, enamelled sleeves for the standard matchbox and the extra large household size were widely produced, and may still be found.

Metal cigar magazines seem to have been less common souvenirs but cigarette boxes and pocket cases are common. Another change in habits is reflected in the ever-increasing variety of makeup containers. In the nineteenth century, the containers were for toilet articles such as cold cream and toothpowder. Gradually, a mirror and comb case became permissible handbag necessities and now ever more ingenious combinations of powder compact, lipstick and eye makeup containers abound. Mirrors, watches or lighters may be incorporated and this is one of the most important sections of the novelty souvenir trade. The majority of such items are imported.

8 ... But It Is a Souvenir

This chapter deals with a wide variety of souvenirs most of which were mass produced by mechanical means. It is intended more as an illustration of Victorian ingenuity than an exhaustive treatment of all types of souvenir not already mentioned.

CELLULOID, 'COMPOSITION', IVORINE AND OTHER ARTIFICIAL MATERIALS

Celluloid, almost the first synthetic thermoplastic material, was created by Alexander Parkes in 1865. He was trying to find a substitute for natural horn which could also be shaped by heat and pressure. Cellulose nitrate, treated with alcohol and camphor, is its basic ingredient and it suffered from a tendency to discolour and become brittle as well as being highly inflammable. Nevertheless it achieved considerable success. From the late 1870s, imitation ivory, jet and tortoiseshell in particular were widely used for personal ornaments and decorative containers. When in doubt, it is usual to cloak one's ignorance as to precisely what they are made of by calling them 'composition', just as today 'plastic' covers a multitude of souvenir sellers' sins from the inflatable legs coat hanger to the bosom cruet or gonk-type horror toy.

Early plastic with the legend 'A present from . . .' appears as a similar range of containers to Mauchline ware. One common feature is the peepshow view in which a clear magnifying lens reveals a group of, usually, six views when the piece is held to the light. Things dec-

Plate 24   Scottish deerhide souvenirs.

orated in this way include pencils and needle cases with the lens in the top, and oval snuffboxes. It seems probable that the device was patented but most examples known to the author would appear to be eastern. Certainly, peepshows in bone or ivory are most likely to be Japanese. Brighton views, including the old chain pier and therefore theoretically not much later than 1896, seem to be the commonest survivors. Miniature binoculars, brooches and keyrings with a similar effect were produced between the wars and more recently ballpoint pens have appeared. Novelties in which the views are of more or less naked ladies are usually of foreign origin, as are the pens in which a lady ecdysist performs.

CRESTED LEATHER GOODS

Since the early 1930s at least, a wide range of good quality leather goods, localised by gold blocked town crests, has been available. As with the early pink ware, most of the items are utilitarian; indeed, they are also supplied plain to sell on their own merits. Apart from subtle changes of shape to follow contemporary fashions, and of interior compartments to accommodate new sizes in banknotes, the 50p piece and credit cards, their designs have varied little. The only aid to dating may be the infiltration of plastic as a replacement for leather or fabric in linings. Most can be described as containers for handbag or pocket and the range is from those for licence or comb to the indiarubber cherished by generations of schoolboys, blazoned on its book-shaped leather case 'To right a wrong by E. Raser'. The largest manufacturer holds 'literally several thousand dies' of town crests. For over forty years, he has managed to combine the use of good quality leather with an ability to produce a reasonably priced,

Plate 25　Crested leather souvenirs.

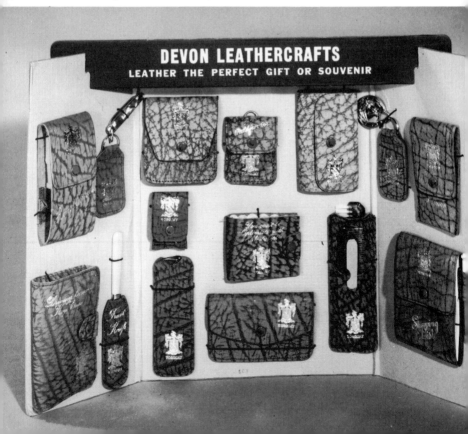

easily-posted non-offensive souvenir and sufficient salesmanship to prevent plastic imitations proving Gresham's law. One wonders if the type will prove as durable as Goss.

GLASS

Paperweights and related glass ornaments with topographical views

Once the heavy tax on glass was repealed, plain glass paper-weights were cheap enough for the souvenir market. It was realised that the traditional concave shape would enhance the effectiveness of a scene painted on the flat base of a plain glass weight and about 1850 transfer-printed views, of the type so characteristic of souvenir wares, appeared. The engraved views were tinted. Favoured colours included a bright green, a brilliant blue and a rich yellow ochre; the decorated surface was covered with a thick protective coat of paint. In the more expensive ranges, a metallic gold increased the liveliness of the reflections, with a particularly attractive effect when used to depict water. As with much Mauchline ware, the pictures are usually merely titled and, because of their reduction to a standard size, are curiously lacking in scale; thus waterfalls appear to be a uniform height, whether they are Niagara or the contrived cascade at some English beauty spot. The quality of the engravings is seldom high. Occasional spelling errors betray the continental origin of most, if not all such objects.

As with the better quality millefiori glass, other items were made in the same technique. These include salt cellars, pin trays and small personal ornaments such as brooches and cufflinks. Weights might be mounted for display in metal stands or the seats of miniature chairs. As with other view wares there was a gradual deterioration in quality with time, scenes being re-engraved without reference to the original. From about 1890, photographic views replace engravings. As on contemporary continental view china, the scenes are still tinted but the characteristic colours seem to alter to pale pinks and blues, and mother-of-pearl replaces the gold backing. Later weights, particu-

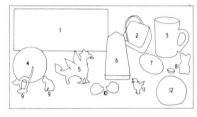

Plate 26 (1) Tunbridge ware-type workbox, about 1900, (2) Irish miniature basket, 1960s, (3) Green mug, glass with enamel decoration, made in Bohemia, 'A present from London', 1890s, (4) Derbyshire alabaster dish, 1960s, (5) Welsh dragon in red-stained wood, 1920s, (6) German paperweight showing St Paul's Cathedral, London, about 1900, (7) Circular paperweight showing Houses of Parliament, London, about 1900, (8) Pottery Manx cat and saucer of cream, 1960s, (9) Lucky black cats in metal (*left*) and wood (*right*), 1950s and about 1900 respectively, (10) Pottery hedgehogs, Isle of Man, 1960s, (11) Cornish chough, glass, 1950s, (12) Paperweight of horse chestnut bud embedded in plastic, Inverness, 1960s.

larly those of the 1920s and 30s, are made from flat slabs of glass and the scenes cease to be transferred. In consequence, while their coats of paint may be chipped or scored, earlier weights are more often found in better condition than later examples which, with glue holding their printed paper backs in position, are at the mercy of every change in humidity.

The range of localities is, as usual with topographical wares, enormous, and the same factories supplied resorts many thousands of miles apart. The author has seen an early salt cellar with a view of a Simla hotel and a pair of flat weights with 1920s views of Heidelberg identical in type with contemporary examples from Weston-super-Mare. Simple view weights are still reasonably plentiful but other items and the earliest engraved scenes are becoming more expensive. Since the scenes in, for example, the cufflinks are virtually identical they were presumably made by the same factories. In the 1919–39 period, 'snowstorm' scenic weights were supplied to the British souvenir market. Modern scenic weights, including a poor imitation of the snowstorm, are almost invariably plastic but glass wall plaques, trays, drip mats and ash trays with applied paper views abound and printed and 'engraved' scenic pieces, particularly attractive rectangular ash trays, are still made.

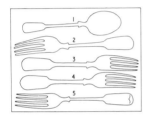

Plate 27 Cutlery by Daniel & Arter, Birmingham, probably late nineteenth century: (2) Japanese Silver, (1, 3, 5) Laxey Silver, (4) Nevada Silver.

Painted and engraved items and glass models

At the very beginning of the period under consideration, the Yarmouth decorator of glass and ceramics, William Absolon, was adding the magic words 'A present from Yarmouth' to his embellishments on glass. Such pieces, usually of poor quality, continued to be produced and might also be further 'personalised' to order by the addition of Christian names. These are most often found on drinking vessels ranging in size from wine glasses to heavy pint tankards. Coloured glass with enamel decoration was imported from the continent, already localised with 'A present from . . .' – a London example, marked 'Made in Bohemia' on its base, is illustrated. As well as engraving names to order, craftsmen with resort shops would also manipulate glass rods to fashion small animals or, for wealthier customers, elaborate ship models. These can hardly be marked, so without a history will be indistinguishable from 'friggers' produced by workmen in larger glass factories and the similar lines produced now as giftwares – most recently distinct because they are fashioned in plastic. Friggers or whigmaleeries seem to have originated as a source of workmen's beer money, being fashioned from the glass left over at the end of the day, but they are so numerous that perhaps the terms may be expanded to cover the whole range of glass fantasies from walking-sticks to spun-glass fountains. It would seem that many resorts had glass blowers as part of their amusements; such workers might have stalls at the seaside in the season and visit fairs and indoor exhibitions elsewhere during the rest of the year.

Pressed glass

The technique by which an effect akin to the results of laborious cutting could be achieved merely by pressing the molten glass with a metal die came to Britain from the USA in the 1830s. At first, it was praised because of its resemblance to cut glass and slavishly imitated the designs appropriate to this. Later, a certain vernacular exuberance

Plate 28 Pressed glass souvenir plate, design apparently adapted from one commemorating Queen Victoria's jubilee, about 1889.

was given free reign and the more mechanised technique was widely used for souvenirs. Vases, often in the form of baskets, in opaque or milky pressed glass might have localising words added in paint. The medium seems to have been used particularly for souvenir plates of Queen Victoria's Jubilee, the Coronation of King Edward VII and Queen Alexandra and, more recently, the Festival of Britain, and the author was beginning to doubt that it had been used for resort souvenir plates. However, she acquired 'A present from the Isle of Man' in which the centre has the island's three-legs emblem and the rim the

Victoria Jubilee floral emblems. The name 'Mary' is clumsily engraved in a space originally reserved for the date, 1887. Comparison with other pieces known to have been purchased at the Isle of Man International Exhibition of 1892 suggests that the transformation is of this date but there is no evidence as to manufacturer.

Silver glass

About the middle of the nineteenth century a method was patented by which a reflecting substance, a solution of silver nitrate, could be enclosed between two layers of glass. This could be used to produce an ornament with all the lustre of metal but which, as well as being much less costly, remained untarnished for a very long period. Such pieces were produced in typical silver shapes, tall amphoræ, goblets, etc but are usually betrayed by the bulbous rims and lack of crisp mouldings even when viewed from a distance. They were, and similar-seeming pieces are, popular as fairground prizes. Typically, they are additionally decorated with opaque paint in floral motifs and bear the inevitable 'A present from . . .' Since personal names and mottos also are frequent it would seem that some were finished to order by retailers. Their main period of fashion as chimney ornaments in unsophisticated homes seems to have been 1850–70. They are often to be found in antique shops but damp has frequently attacked the silvering, usually because the disc plugging the hole in the base is no longer securely fastened. Good pieces are marked 'Hale Thomson's patent London', or by the main licensee 'Varnish & Co', or with the range name 'Elfin', but all souvenir pieces seen have been unmarked. While the original firms ceased to sell such items in the market for high quality ornamental glass it would appear that the process has been revived from time to time by the souvenir manufacturers.

LOCAL PERFUMES

Floral scent, ' . . . the most acceptable Souvenir that can be presented to a friend . . .' was popular throughout the period under consideration. Resort chemists, who also put up their own medicinal prescriptions and lotions, would, with the aid of a vivid imagination to invent an appealing name, create their own local perfumes. Thus the enterprising Mr Payne of Cowes exhibited his Royal Osborne Bouquet at the Great Exhibition, together with soap containing Isle of Wight sand and 'an exquisite condiment' called Royal Osborne sauce. Since almost every chemist would have his own creation, those offered in the Isle of Man will be used to illustrate the style of name and advertising.

The earliest, dating from about 1852, seems to have been 'Greensill's Original MONA BOUQUET . . . combining all the fragrant properties of Mona's choicest flowers . . . No visitor should return without a Bottle of this Esprit!'. It proved the most successful of the Manx scents and was widely sold on the island and by a few mainland stockists, notably in Liverpool and London. Surviving nineteenth century bottles are moulded clear glass with a printed black-on-white label of the type used commonly by chemists on prescriptions, although the type styles are more florid than is now usual. It is a sweet, unsophisticated scent, to modern noses suggesting those favoured by toiletry manufacturers, but fading quite attractively. Its trademark is 'The Tower of Refuge, Douglas Bay . . . without which it will be spurious'. It is still available, in a slim fluted bottle and a light orange box with a reproduction of the original style of label. A copy of an early advertisement is used as packing.

Imitation is said to be the sincerest form of flattery and it is one much practised by the souvenir trade. There was soon a rival Mona Bouquet, 'Turner's True, Original and Genuine . . . By appointment to HRH Prince Leopold, registered title number 32,388.' This was advertised beside the same firm's Manx Fairy, 'Mona's choicest perfume', registered title number 32,386 – also the name of a popular contemporary excursion boat. Douglas Bowman's had Isle of Man Bouquet and at the Apothecaries' Hall A. Wilson would sell you Manx Wild Flowers. Kermode's, the main chemist in the south,

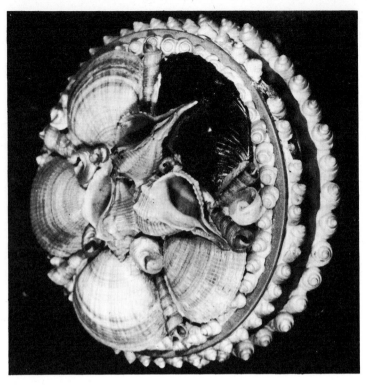

Plate 29 Shellwork box typical of those imported by Marcus Samuel in the nine-teenth century; species include rayed trough, smooth cockle, whelk, and tops – not-ably the much-favoured small pearly species.

offered Manx Gem in Castletown. Visitors to the northern resort of Ramsey had a wider choice from Pallister's Albert Tower Bouquet or Ellan Vannin (literally 'dearest isle', an affectionate patriotic name for the Isle of Man), priced in 1875 at 1s 6d or 2s 6d a bottle, or Priestland's Mannin Beg Bouquet or MHK Bouquet. (MHK is the standard abbreviation of Member of the House of Keys, the official style of members of the lower house of Tynwald, the Manx parlia-ment.) Peel, the sunset city, was not outdone, since Thomas Lawrence had created a Fenella Bouquet, named in honour of the Walter Scott heroine associated with its castle.

The prices mentioned indicate that scent was among the more expensive souvenirs; a printed handkerchief, for example, was 6½d and small gold and silver brooches and pins 6d and 1s. While scent is essentially fleeting, early bottles do sometimes survive with their labels intact and the warring advertisements in old guide books make amusing reading. A few, like Mona Bouquet, have survived the years and since the 1950s a number of producers have emulated their tradition and created local scents. This is particularly true of Ireland and Scotland. There are also a few perfumes based on locally-distilled essences. However, the souvenir perfume industry is now largely in the hands of sizeable firms whose products, of which violet scents seem the most conspicuous, are localised largely by labelling and much of the attractiveness is contained in the elaborate packaging. The cost is usually reasonable and, since scent can be offered as a present without regard to age group or degree of affection, it remains popular.

TEXTILES

Embroidery designs

Embroidery was popular throughout the period under consideration and many women would wish to give their work some special touch to remind them of their holidays. Firms produced designs to cater for this from an early date. Some were commissioned but others were on general sale. The Manx Museum has a design 'for beadwork or worsted', published by Ackerman's of London in 1836, showing the three-legs emblem of the Isle of Man in carefully shaded detail. More recently it has acquired a panel worked in England from an identical pattern. Early nineteenth century directories show that most resorts had shops selling needlework requisites. When the prolific publishers of Berlin woolwork patterns produced one of a local scene or emblem it would doubtless be seized on with delight by both the shopkeeper and her public. Embroiderers also made their own designs, often with the aid of books of views or picture postcards. At the end of the eighteenth century there was a fashion for imitating etchings in black silk on sarcenet, and a view of Lincoln Cathedral in this style was exhibited as late as 1851, when the pieces displayed by F.U. Tanner of Bühler, Appenzell, Switzerland at the Great Exhibition helped to extend the fashion for another forty years.

This long-popular style of embroidery enjoyed a new lease of life when in 1935 William Briggs & Co Ltd of Manchester started issuing packs of needlework etchings under their Penelope label. The designs were, and are, stamped on good quality fabric and black thread is provided to complete the work. Abbeys, castles, cathedrals and places of interest such as Burns' Cottage, Ann Hathaway's Cottage and Shakespeare's birthplace are depicted. At one time there were some four hundred different designs but with the decline in hand embroidery, resulting partly from the influence of television since many women cannot view and sew, there are now only forty-five. However, the range is not static, with both the new Liverpool Roman Catholic and Coventry cathedrals already represented. It is interesting to see which designs have stood the test of time. Not surprisingly, there are eight London views, the same number of Scottish, the obligatory Shakespeare country sights already mentioned and the ever-popular Kenilworth and Warwick; but why should the tiny Isle of Man retain four (out of its original five) and its map?

Printed handkerchiefs

Just as the repeal of the tax on glass made possible the introduction of inexpensive souvenir paperweights, so in 1831 the lifting of restrictions on printed goods made possible the production of cheap printed souvenir handkerchiefs. These were made from both silk and cotton and it appears that individual shops commissioned exclusive designs. Thus in 1868 the proprietor of Faulkener's Bazaar in Douglas (so successful an enterprise that it met the chronic shortage of small change by issuing its own tokens) offered:

> ... Specialities for visitors ... Manx pictorial handkerchiefs ... Which he has had expressly produced for his own trade ... The design consists of the Manx Arms and Motto in the centre, with finely engraved Views of Douglas, Ramsey, Castletown and Peel Island and Castle – at each corner on silk plain 2s 6d twilled 3s 6d.

This proved a popular line and by 1882 the rival firm of Cottier & Cubbon had an extensive range of ' . . . Fancy goods suitable for presents. Manx handkerchiefs. Including the Manx Puzzle, The Tourist, Manx Cat, Views of Douglas and Country, the Map, the Steamer, Port Skillion, The Pictorial Legs &c'. The earlier examples clearly drew on the repertoire of designs used on other view wares and are usually monochrome, dark red, green, blue or black.

Since commemorative, patriotic and political handkerchiefs abound it is apparent that most were produced by specialist firms, presumably with the same roller-printing presses used in the production of other contemporary printed textiles. The author has seen examples in which the ornamental border is faulty because the handkerchiefs selected for printing had the characteristic cording found on undecorated examples. This would suggest that some souvenir handkerchiefs, like some of the printed fabric programmes beloved of Victorian theatregoers, were locally produced on ordinary hand presses using printer's ink. This assumption is reinforced by the fact that both the Isle of Man map vignettes and a satirical political cartoon 'King Orry on his Tynwald Mount' – in which all the figures have three legs and the members of the House of Keys appear as door keys – are known both printed on paper and on handkerchiefs. The only known handkerchief printing factory, near Douglas, had closed by 1780 so it seems likely that some local printers of newspapers and guide books were responsible for the handkerchiefs.

Appendix 1
Major Coastal Resorts

The list comprises basically those resorts advertising in the popular press in spring 1973.

Resorts are listed alphabetically by counties.

Some small resorts are included because their souvenirs are common; a virtually uninhabited place will sell large numbers of souvenirs if it is a stop on a standard tour itinerary. Otherwise, places listed are mainly large towns with the usual amenities of promenade with boarding houses, pier, and entertainments.

To give an idea of the period of development, and a foundation for a quick comparison with the towns the visitor knows today, information has been abstracted from sources including Mavor's *The British Tourist* (1798) and *Seaside Watering Places* (1895) and presented in code form.

KEY

Example: (name of resort) m * R P S(L)(LP) +

m	entry in *The British Tourist* (1798); paucity of entries reflects late eighteenth century lack of interest in coastal resorts
*	entry in *Seaside Watering Places* (1895)
R	railway station within two miles (in 1895)
P	pier
S	steamer service carrying visitors to resort (in 1895) from . . .
L	London
LP	Liverpool
+	population in 1895 listed as over 10,000

Avon
Clevedon * R P(built 1869, collapsed 1970s); Portishead *; Weston-super-Mare * R P(two)

Clwyd
Colwyn Bay * R P S(LP) (to Llandudno)

Cornwall
Bude *; Falmouth * R; Fowey * R; Hayle; Land's End; Looe *; Marazion and St Michael's Mount *; Newlyn; Newquay * R; Perranporth * R; Penzance * R; St Agnes *; St Ives * R; Tintagel and Boscastle * R

Cumbria
Grange-over-Sands * R (has remained almost static in size)

Devon
Barnstaple; Brixham * R; Budleigh Salterton *; Clovelly *; Combe Martin * (reputed to be 'the longest village in England'); Croyde Bay; Dawlish *; Exmouth *; Ilfracombe * R S(daily packet from Bristol) P; Lynton and Lynmouth *; Paignton * R P; Plymouth * R; Salcombe * S(packet from London via Plymouth) (original site for George IV's marine pavilion); Seaton and Sidmouth * R (Jasper, agate chalcedony, cornelian on beach; rare zoophytes and ferns); Teignmouth * R P; Torquay * R P; Westward Ho! * R (founded formally as a resort 1863); Woolacombe and Morthoe * R

Dorset
Bournemouth * R P(replacing earlier extensible pier); Charmouth * (noted for fossils); Christchurch; Highcliffe; Lyme Regis m * (noted for fossils); Poole; Swanage * R; Weymouth m * R

Dyfed
Aberystwyth m R P ('It has long . . . been a favoured sea-bathing place'.); Llanelli R

East Sussex
Bexhill-on-Sea * R; Brighton and Hove * R P(chain pier 1823–96, marine palace and pier 1901, West pier); Eastbourne * R P +; Hastings and St Leonards * R P; Newhaven * R; Seaford * R

Essex
Clacton-on-Sea * R P(1873; pavilion 1890s); Frinton-on-Sea * R; Southend-on-Sea * R S(L) P

Gwynedd
Barmouth m * ('It has long been admired and frequented as a bathing place.'); Llandudno * R P S(LP); Pwllheli *

Hampshire
Hayling Island * R; Lee-on-Solent * R; Portsmouth and Southsea m * R

Humberside
Bridlington * R; Cleethorpes * R P(1870); Hornsea m * R

Isle of Wight
Bembridge *; Bonchurch *; Brading *; Cowes *; Freshwater *; Ryde * P (old tramway and railway); Sandown *; Seaview *; Shanklin and Totland Bay*; Ventnor *; Yarmouth *

Queen Victoria made the island fashionable by her constant use of Osborne House, her residence near Cowes.

Peculiarly local souvenirs include coloured sands, and cork items which though ostensibly made from local cork oaks are in fact imported.

Kent
Broadstairs * R; Deal and Walmer * R P(concrete, Deal); Folkestone; Herne Bay * R P(1873, subsequently extended); Margate * R S(L) P +; Ramsgate * R (day trips to Boulogne 6s return in 1895)

Lancashire
Blackpool * R P(three) +; Lytham St Annes * R P(1885, pavilion 1904); Morecambe * R P

Lincolnshire
Skegness * R (noted for botanical opportunities)

Merseyside
New Brighton * P S(LP) (regular ferry); Southport * R P +

Mid Glamorgan
Porthcawl *

Norfolk
Cromer and Sheringham * R P(Cromer, 1901); Great Yarmouth * R P(two); Hunstanton * R

North Yorkshire
Filey * R; Scarborough m * R; Whitby m * R

Somerset
Blue Anchor *; Burnham-on-Sea * R P(unfinished); Minehead; Porlock; Portishead *; Sand Bay (modern); Watchet *

Suffolk
Felixstowe * R P(1904); Lowestoft and Oulton Broad * R P(three, Lowestoft)

West Sussex
Bognor (Regis from 1924) * R P(1865); Littlehampton * R; Shoreham-by-Sea * R; Worthing * R P +

SCOTLAND

The growth of Scottish coastal resorts did not follow the English pattern and they are therefore not included in the list. Among early destinations for steamer-borne trippers from Glasgow's Broomielaw were Helensburgh, Largs and Rothesay. Portobello received Edinburgh's excursionists and there was resort development on the North Berwick and Ayrshire shores, the latter accessible from both cities. Oban can claim to be a resort in the English sense. Hydropathic hotels such as those at Dunblane, Gleneagles and Pitlochry, and the spa at Strathpeffer, catered for middle-class visitors.

ISLE OF MAN

The principal resorts are:

Castletown   Lacks residential accommodation but much visited, initially for Castle Rushen and, up to 1973, the Witches Mill museum of witchcraft and superstition.

Douglas   Steamers from Greenock and Liverpool from early nineteenth century, main building of boarding houses in late 1860s.

Laxey   'The world's largest waterwheel', named the Lady Isabella, was and is a major attraction.

Peel   Main attractions: castle and kipper factories.

Port Erin and Port St Mary   Small resort with late nineteenth/early twentieth century developments.

Ramsey   'Royal' after Queen Victoria's visit; Queen's Pier used by steamers.

Appendix 2
Registration Marks

Under the Registration Act of 1842, designs could be registered to protect the manufacturer against unscrupulous rivals. Many souvenirs, including some of foreign manufacture, bear the lozenge mark with a letter code indicating day, month, and year of registration. After 1884, the code was changed to a number alone.

Class of manufacture	I	metal	II	wood
(in top compartment)	III	glass	IV	pottery

1842–67	year letter below class left hand corner— month	right hand corner—day manufacturer's code at foot	
1868–83	right hand corner—year left hand corner— manufacturer's mark	day below class month at foot	

Year letters								
	1842	X	1853	Y	1864	N	1874	U
	43	H	54	J	65	W	75	S
	44	C	55	E	66	Q	76	V
	45	A	56	L	67	T	77	P
	46	I	57	K	68	X	78	D
	47	F	58	B	69	H	79	Y
	48	U	59	M	70	C	80	J
	49	S	60	Z	71	A	81	E
	50	V	61	R	72	I	82	L
	51	P	62	O	73	F	83	K
	52	D	63	G				

Month letters							
Jan C	Feb G	Mar W	Apr H	May E	Jun M		
July I	Aug R	Sep D	Oct B	Nov K	Dec A		

Appendix 3
Wooden Souvenirs

T—Tunbridge ware   M—Mauchline ware
A—arbutus and bog oak

Desk accessories

Item	T M A	Item	T M A
Blotters, book or case	T M A	Letter racks	M A
hand	M A	Paper knives	T M A
Book covers	M A	weights	M A
marks	T M	Pencils	T M A
rests and slides	T A	Pen holders	T M A
Boxes, book	T A	stands	T M A
desk accessory	T A	trays	T M A
drawing material	T	Pen wipers	T M A
painting material	T	Rulers	T M A
pen/pencil	T M A	Sealing wax outfits	T
seal	T	Stationery cabinets	T
stamp	T M A	racks	M A
Cases for compasses	T	Writing boxes	T A
Indiarubber holders	M	desks	T A
Inkstands	T M A		

Household and ornamental

Item	T M A	Item	T M A
Albums, photograph	T M A	Egg stands	M A
Boxes for cigarettes	T M A	timers	M A
letters (hall)	M A	Finger plates	M
matches	T M A	Frames (picture, photo)	T M A

	T	M	A		T	M	A
money	T	M	A	Fruit knives		M	A
photographs		M		Hearth brushes		M	
postcards	T			Kettle holders	T		
spices	T			Match stands	T	M	
				Newspaper rests	T		
Caddy spoons	T		A	Pictures, mosaic	T		
Cake baskets	T	M		Quaiches		M	
Calendars (perpetual)		M	A	Salad spoons/forks	T		A
Candle arms	T		A	Screens	T		A
stands	T		A	Serviette rings	T	M	A
sticks	T	M	A	Spill vases/holders	T	M	A
Cases for bottles			A	Sprinkler eggs		M	
lancets			A	String holders	T	M	A
glasses (med.)			A	Tables	T		A
thermometers			A	Taper holders	T		A
tapers	T	M	A	Tea caddies	T	M	A
Chairs	T		A	Tea poys	T		
Chests, medicine	T			Thermometer stands	T	M	
miniature	T			Tobacco barrels	T		A
Coasters		M		Trays, general purpose	T		A
Cabinets (coin)	T			for visiting cards		M	A
Egg cups		M	A	Vases, traditional		M	A
				cauldron shaped		M	A

Personal objects

	T	M	A		T	M	A
Bracelets			A	Necklaces			A
Brooches	T	M	A	Notebooks and cases	T	M	
Buttons, Breadalbane		M		Ornaments, hair			A
other			A	Parasol handles		M	A
Cases, card	T	M	A	Pendants			A
cheroot	T	M		Pipes			A
cigar		M		Purses		M	
cigarette (late)	T			Reticule frames	T		

Crosses, pendant	A	Smelling salts bottle	
standing	A	cases	M
Earrings	A	Snuffboxes	T M A
Etuis	T M	Sovereign boxes	T
Hatpin heads	T A	Spectacle cases	T M
Matchboxes	M A	Watch chains	A
Memo tablets	T M		

Sewing aids

Boxes, button	M A	Emery cushions	T
cotton	M	Knitting needle protectors	T
needle	T	sheaths	T
pin	T	Ladies' companions	M
reel	T	Needlework clamps	T
scissors	T M	Pin cushions	T M A
Cases, bodkin	M	poppets	T M A
crochet hook	M	Sewing compendiums	T
knitting needle	M	Silk winders	T M A
needle	M	Thread holders for balls	T M
thimble	T M A	skeins	T
Darning blocks, glove	T	Tape measures, novelty	T M A
other	M	Tatting shuttles	M A
Darning eggs	T M A	Thread barrels	T M
mushrooms	M	waxers	T M
Ell rules	T	Workboxes	T M A

Toilet accessories

Bonnet stands	T	Clothes brush backs	T M A
Boxes, cold cream	M	Glove stretchers	M A
glove	T M A	Hair brush backs	M A
handkerchief	T M A	tidies	M
hairpin	T M A	Mirror frames	T A

jewellery	T M A	Pin trays	T M A	
lipsalve	M	Ring stands	T A	
ring	T M	Toilet boxes, fitted	T A	
rouge	T M	Trinket stands	T	
stud	T M A	trays	A	
tiepin	M A	Watch stands, plain	M A	
tooth powder	M	with stud		
Cases, pomatum	M	tray	T	
scent	M	Razor strops and hones	M	
adhesive plaster	M			

Toys and games

Banjo	T	Boxes, puzzle	T M	
Bilboquet	T	trick opening	T	
Boards, backgammon	T A	Markers for games	T M A	
chess	A	Miniature furniture, etc	T M A	
cribbage	T A	Organ cases	T	
Pope Joan	T	Skipping rope handles	M	
counters	T M A	Spinning tops	T M	
Boxes, game	T	Yoyos	T	
playing card	T M A			

Appendix 4
Geological Jewellery

Table 1: east coast resorts mentioned in *Seaside Watering Places* (1895) as places where semi-precious stones may be found.

	agate	amber	cornelian	jet	others
Runswick				*	
Whitby				*1	
Withernsea	*	*	*	*	
Cromer		*		*	*
Southwold	*		*		
Aldborough	*	*	*	*	
Felixstowe		*	*		
Harwich		*2			

1 'Jet ornaments may be obtained cheaply, with an almost boundless choice. It is an easy matter to obtain access to the workshops where they are made.'
2 Harwich specialised in amber-set rings prior to the mid 1840s.

Table 2: other resorts where semi-precious stones are stated to occur.

	agate	moss agate	cornelian	chalcedony	jasper	amethyst	citrine
Folkestone			*				
Sidmouth	*		*	*	*		
Budleigh Salterton		*		*			
Marazion 'crystal beach'						*	*

St Buryan				*	*
Lamorna Cove				*	*
Sennen Cove				*	*
Clevedon[1]			*		
Sandown	*	*			
Peel and Pt of Ayre, IoM[2]	*	*		*	

1 Specimens in Weston-super-Mare Museum.
2 Specimens in the Manx Museum, Douglas.

Appendix 5 Firms Making Armorial China: Provisional List

This list is basically that of trade marks noted by the author, and is not exhaustive. Identification of English firms was made by Stoke-on-Trent Museum; the dates given are those when the marks were used and may not correspond to the period of production of giftwares.

ARCADIAN CHINA, A & S Arkinstall & Sons Ltd, Trent Bridge Pottery, Stoke-on-Trent, 1904–24, mark: helmet with mantlings above a globe.

CARLTON CHINA, W & R Wiltshaw & Robinson Ltd, Carlton Works, Stoke-on-Trent, 1925–57, became CARLTON WARE in 1958, still make giftwares.

W.H. GOSS London Road and Eastwood Vale, Stoke-on-Trent, armorial china 1880s–1940, life of firm 1858–1944, mark: 'a goshawk ducally gorged'.

GRAFTON CHINA, ABJ & SONS LTD A.B. Jones & Sons, Grafton Works, Stoke-on-Trent, now CROWN LYNN CERAMICS (UK) LTD, mark: eyed sun rising above shield bearing Staffordshire knot.

DAINTY WARE, E.B. & CO ⎫ Evidence suggests that
FLORENTINE CHINA ⎬ these are British firms,
MILTON CHINA ⎭ probably twentieth century.

NORNESFORD CHINA Nornesford Ltd, Commerce Street, Longton, Stoke-on-Trent, 1920 on, made interesting figure models.

QUEEN'S CHINA George Warrilow & Sons Ltd, Queen's Pottery, Longton, Stoke-on-Trent, 1887–1940.

SAVOY CHINA, B R & CO Birks, Rawlins & Co Ltd, Vine Pottery, Stoke-on-Trent, 1900–33

SHELLEY Shelley Potteries Ltd, The Foley, Longton, Stoke-on-Trent, and Wileman & Co, Foley Potteries.

SUSSEX CHINA, S P & CO Possibly Sylvan Pottery, Hanley, Stoke-on-Trent, but this is a post-1946 use of the name.

SWAN CHINA Charles Ford, Cannon St, Stoke-on-Trent, 1874–1904.

VICTORIA Cartwright & Edwards (also used by Czech firm, Gemma).

WILLOW ART Hewitt & Leadbetter, Willow Pottery, Longton, Stoke-on-Trent, 1907–19, made some interesting figure models including three-legged dog 'Prince Toby Orry' to order of a Manx firm (design copied from postcard).

Continental firms
Most imported souvenirs, if not unmarked, bear only the name of their country of origin.

BEMMA, MADE IN CZECHOSLOVAKIA Faulty rendering of GEMMA?

GEMMA Schmidt & Co, Victoria Porcelain Factory, Altrohlau, Bohemia, owned by Lazarus & Rosenfeld, London. Founded 1883. Mark: GEMMA diagonally on shield under crown, MADE IN CZECHOSLOVAKIA in green underglaze. Easily the most abundant marked continental armorial souvenirs.

ROYAL COBURG Probably used by Albert Riemann's Bohemian factory, founded 1860, mark: COBURG 1860 (beneath mitre in 1920s).

JULIUS GREINER SONS Lauscha, Sachsen-Meiningen, Thuringia, founded 1871, specialists like GEMMA in 'Elfenbeinminiaturen', 'ivory' miniatures – may have produced some of the unmarked pieces. At least one Manx firm ordered exclusive lines from a firm of this name in the period 1920–35.

Appendix 6
Ceramic Souvenir Types

GENERAL

Pieces recorded here are thought to be pre-1910 and, unless otherwise indicated, of continental origin. Goss-type crested wares and pink ware are covered elsewhere in appendices and text and do not appear below. Indications of rarity usually relate to type and should not be regarded as definitive, since the products of more than one manufacturer may be involved. The localities cited are those on pieces seen by the author.

Emendations welcomed.

BOWLS

1 Deep rich blue, with gilt, 3 feet (sometimes pierced), coloured view on upper half, approx diameter at rim 4in, localised *Douglas*, fairly common, similar VASES, JUG.

2 White, hand-coloured transfer-printed view, diameter 3in, marked SHELLEY CHINA, ENGLAND, *Castletown*, fairly common.

3 White, coloured picture of three-legged man, gilt legend, diameter 4in, possibly German, *Isle of Man*, rare.

4 Orange lustre, hand-tinted, black transfer-printed view, approx diameter 5in, marked FOREIGN, probably related to pink ware, *Symon's* (sic) *Yat,* common.

BOXES

1 Conta & Boehme fairing-type boxes may be localised by inscriptions: girl and puppy, *Aberdeen, Abergavenny*; steam engine, *Blackpool*; girl and lamb, *Ely*; paddle steamer, *Liverpool to Menai Straits*; puppy

with umbrella, *Milford Haven*. (Conta & Boehme products are usually numbered.)

More rarely, subjects themselves may be localised.

Specifically Manx:

2 Laxey wheel, uncommon.

3 Three-legged man, fairing-type with variable hand-painted decoration on white ground, often with boot black, captioned 'Lor, three legs, I'll charge 2d', fairly common.

4 As above, in self-coloured Parian-type body, rare.

5 As above, 1920s, known as a 'Hi, Kelly', manufacturer possibly Greiner, should be common.

6 Pink and green with gilt, gilt roses overpainted, 4in × 2in, arms surrounded by raised gilt, *Douglas*; matching items include PIN TRAY and WATCH POCKET, suggesting manufactere also of DRESSING TABLE SETS; fairly common.

7 White, small hand-painted flowers, circular, brass hinges and rim, approx diameter 2½in, exists as SNUFFBOX, *Douglas*, fairly common.

Welsh types:

8 Fairing type, *Ladies of Llangollen*, common; post-1918 types also common, some marked MADE IN JAPAN; like 'Hi Kelly', commissioned from postcard design.

9 *Welsh tea party, Welsh farmer's daughter*, figures wear black steeple hats and red petticoats, may turn up localised for non-Welsh resorts, common.

CANDLESTICKS

1 White chamber-type, hand-painted flowers, gilt legend, diameter 6in, later examples probably Czechoslovakian, *Douglas*, common.

2 Plain upright stick, white, hand-painted flowers, gilt legend, height 6in, *Douglas*, common.

3 Moulded scroll feet, wax tray leaf-shaped, white, hand-painted flowers, gilt legend, diameter 5in approx, *Douglas*, common.

A pre-1910 date is suggested for candlesticks 1–3 since they are basic utilitarian shapes, whereas post-1920 souvenir candlesticks tend to be less functional.

CANISTER

1 Standard Goss armorial shape, height 3in, but with black transfer-printed view, marked w.h. goss, *Peel*, uncommon.

CUPS AND SAUCERS

(Teacup size unless stated otherwise)

1 White, moulded scrolls cartouche, much gilt, *Brighton*, common.

2 Pearly white ground with 'willow pattern blue' fern design and gilt, coffee size, *Douglas*, possibly English, uncommon.

3 Dark pink, panels of Chinese-style figures, gilt legend, coffee size, marked FOREIGN, possibly related to pink ware but more probably oriental, *Douglas*, uncommon.

4 White ground with blue Delft-style hand-painted decoration, lithophane of *Douglas Bay* in base of coffee size cups, apparently rare.

5 White, blue, red and gilt floral design, gilt legend *Isle of Man*, rather small and shallow, possibly 1930s, fairly common.

6 White, fluted, with some orange lustre, probably related to pink ware, *Llandudno*, common.

7 White, gilt moulded swags, dark brown photographic view, gilt legend, MADE IN GERMANY, common.

8 White inside, emerald green outside, gilt legend, *Southport*, common.

9 White, turquoise lining, small flowers, *Southport*, common.

10 White, fluted, gilt legend surrounded by applied moulded flowers, coffee size, possibly English about 1900, *Weston-super-Mare*, uncommon.

11 White, Belleek-type pearly lustre, *Weymouth*, common; also occurs with coloured view and body moulded in pattern of scales.

CRUET

1 White, often with pearly lustre, tinted views, *Douglas*, common; similarly decorated VASES.

DRESSING TABLE SET

1 White, hand-painted flowers, gilt legend, mainly post-1910, Czechoslovakian, uncommon with all pieces perfect.

JUGS

1 Coarse ware, dark blue glaze with gilt, hand-coloured transfer, height 4in, *Laxey*, common.

2 White, Belleek-type lustre on shell-patterned body, tinted picture. Topographical views exist. Welsh lady in steeple hat and red petticoats may be localised for non-Welsh resorts; *Llandudno*; also CUP AND SAUCER, ONE-PERSON TEAPOT, SUGAR BOWL. Common, possibly because revived in 1920s, but complete set seldom found.

3 Staffordshire creamware with black transfer-printed view, about 1789 on, body shape altered in later types, practical sizes and contemporary shapes; may carry transfer patterns similar to rest of pottery's products, eg formalised apples below rim; later pieces often marked with name of retailer who commissioned design; becoming rare as quality recognised; *Brighton*, *Liverpool*, *Ramsey*, etc; also MUGS.

1 Porcelain, transfer-printed in red, Spode, *Brighton*, uncommon.

2 Porcelain, transfer-printed in sepia, hand-painted flowers, *Douglas*, possibly from a pink ware factory, possibly early, uncommon.

3 Porcelain, hand-painted bunches of flowers round puce cartouche, entwined flowers inside rim, made Lowestoft about 1795, *Lowestoft*, rare.

4 White coarse ware, three coloured views within sepia shamrock, possibly Japanese and post-1918, *Durham*, uncommon.

5 White coarse ware, heavily moulded lip, gilt round dark brown photographic view, MADE IN GERMANY, *Holyhead*, common.

6 Earthenware, transfer-printed blue, *Walmer*, fairly common.

7 Earthenware, transfer-printed in black with legend and verse 'From Rocks and Sands and all that's ill May God preserve the Vessel still', about 1790, *Yarmouth*, uncommon in good condition.

PLAQUES

1 Green cabbage leaf style, heart-shaped view panel, marked B & K LTD (Barkers & Kent Ltd – firm ceased operation in 1941), *Glen Helen*, uncommon.

2 Green jasper-like body with white design, 5in × 8in, *Laxey Wheel*, fairly common.

Ann Hathaway's cottage and circular plaques also reported, including pairs of Manx views. Blue and pink jasper grounds are known, as is a hatpin with the three-legs emblem on blue jasper ground. If piece carries a number in the hundreds, it is possibly Conta & Boehme.

3 Dark brown ground, gilt lining, black photographic views, RIDGWAY ENGLAND, commissioned by 'Clague's China Shop, Douglas', *Old Kirk Braddan*; CHEESE DISHES, JUGS, CUPS known, other

household wares probably exist; late nineteenth century, fairly common.

PLATES

1 Porcelain, hand-painted oriental design and (later) gilt legends, diameter 9in, possibly post-1918, Japanese, *Douglas,* common in poor condition.

2 White porcelain with splashy hand-painted flowers and gilt legend, 9in, mainly post-1920 Czechoslovakian, some marked MADE IN AUSTRIA, *Douglas*, common in poor condition. DRESSING TABLE SETS exist.

3 Coloured floral relief decoration and gilt, gilt legend, 9in, FOREIGN, common.

4 RIBBON PLATES with pierced rims, usually 9in but later examples with coloured views may be smaller; later examples with hand-painted flowers may be Czechoslovakian – may have piercing in star or other geometrical shape; also MADE IN AUSTRIA; common, often in poor state.

TEAPOTS

1 White porcelain with ripple moulding and faintly pearly glaze, coloured photographic views (cf ripple-moulded pink ware), marked s beneath coronet, made by P. Donath, Silesia, *Castletown*, uncommon. Sometimes sold as Spode.

2 Staffordshire majolica, three designs exist based on the Manx three-legged man: sailor with rope's end, rare; sailor with ensign, fairly common; man astride tree trunk, uncommon; probably made by William Brownfield's works, Cobridge; Ann Hathaway's cottage exists as a teapot but many other such models are later.

3 Thuringian copy of Staffordshire three-legged man astride tree (see above), late, *Douglas*, rare.

149

TEAPOT STAND

1 White china, transfer-printed flowers, gilt legend, common.

VASE SETS

1 White porcelain, gilt top, tinted photographic view, two small, one large, *Brighton*.

2 Similar to above but whole vase tinted deep green except for view area, thin, *Douglas*, common.

PINK WARE

Information about the manufacture of pink ware is extremely difficult to find and the following list of types is based on the author's observation; it should be accepted only as a general guide.

SHAPES

CUP AND SAUCER Fairly shallow bowl shape, occurs in breakfast size, fairly common for most resorts; souvenirs of continental resorts often have deeper tulip shape.

EGG CUPS Usually plain, uncommon.

JUGS Usually plain, bulbous curves, fairly common.

MUGS Usually fairly straight-sided beakers with handles; miniature and handle-less types exist but are less common.

PLATES Plain dinner plates common, pierced ribbon plates less so, soup plates uncommon as are smaller plates and shapes other than round.

SUGAR BOWLS Plain, shallow, fairly common.

TEAPOTS Plain, or fairly plain, good size, uncommon.

ORNAMENTS such as candlesticks exist.

TYPES

PLAIN TABLE WARES Simple shapes, ground colour is pink lustre, decoration
varies: with gilt legend only
     black transfer-print and legend
     coloured transfer print and legend
     coloured photographic view and legend (late)

MOULDED BODIES Fluted, or twisted ripples, running longitudinally, all-over scales and similar patterns, reserved panels and swags.

APPLIED DECORATION Moulded flowers around legend.

Bibliography

1 SOUVENIRS: A HISTORICAL PERSPECTIVE

CONTEMPORARY BACKGROUND MATERIAL

This includes an enormous diversity of guide books and local newspapers as well as directories such as Pigot's and Slater's. Manx newspapers have been sampled for June, July and August at ten year
intervals from 1800–1920, and similar periods checked for South
Devon and Southport. Directories studied include primarily those
which include the Isle of Man 1824–97, and reference made to advertisements in publications as varied as the Ward Locke guides and the
catalogue of the Isle of Man International Exhibition 1892.

GENERAL GUIDES

Blanchard, E.L. *Adam's Illustrated Descriptive Guide to the Watering
Places*, 1859
Britton, J. and Brayley, E.W. *Beauties of England*, 1802
Head, Sir George *A Home Tour*, 1840–1 etc
Mavor's *The British Tourist*, 1798
Seaside Watering Places, 1895

HISTORICAL BACKGROUND

Hern, A. *The Seaside Holiday*, 1967
Jewitt, R.L.P. *Discovering Spas*, 1971
Lindley, K. *Seaside Architecture*, 1973
Manning-Saunders, R. *Seaside England*, 1951
Marsden, C. *The English at the Seaside*, 1947
Moir, E. *The Discovery of Britain*, 1964
Smith, A. *Beside the Seaside*, 1973

A modern guide useful for locating and identifying resorts is *The AA
Book of the Seaside*, 1973

GENERAL BOOKS ON VICTORIANA

Douglas, J. *Collectable Things*, 1961
Latham, J. *Victoriana*, 1971
Peter, Mary *Collecting Victoriana*, 1965
Woodhouse, C.P. *The Victoriana Collector's Handbook*, 1970

PILGRIMS' BADGES AND SCALLOP SHELLS

Hugo, T. 'Notes on a Collection of Pilgrims' Signs', *Archaeologia*, 38, i (1859), 128–34
Medieval London, the catalogue of the London Museum
Woledge, B. *The Scallop*, 1957

2 WOODWARE

Boothroyd, A.E. *Fascinating Walking Sticks*, 1970 and 1973
Buist, J.S. 'Souvenirs in Wood – Mauchline Ware and the Enterprising Smiths', *Scots Magazine*, 95, vii (1971), 340–7
Pinto, E.H. and E.R. *Tunbridge Ware and Scottish Souvenir Woodware*, 1970

3 FURTHER SOUVENIRS MADE FROM NATURAL MATERIALS

See books listed under 1.

4 GEOLOGICAL SOUVENIRS

Art Journal, Account of Hall's Derbyshire spar works, Sept 1850
Andrew, K.M. 'Stones for the Curlers', *Scots Magazine*, 97, 2 (1972), 418–26
Cray, P. *Coloured Sands of Alum Bay* (official guide), 1969
Firsoff, V.A. *Gemstones of the British Isles*, 1971 (records many traditional localities of semi-precious stones and illustrates worked examples)
Francis, J.G. *Beach Rambles in Search of Seaside Pebbles and Crystals*, 1861
Highlands & Islands Development Board, *Buyer's Guide to Retail Products of the Highlands and Islands*

Kendall, H.P. *The Story of Whitby Jet*, 1936

Official illustrated catalogue of the Great Exhibition, London, 1851

5 JEWELLERY

Art Journal catalogue of the Dublin Exhibition, 1853

Bradford, E. *English Victorian Jewellery*, 1959

Cooper, D. and Battershill, N. *Victorian Sentimental Jewellery*, 1972

Flower, Margaret *Victorian Jewellery*, 1951

Johnson, E. *Description of the Reproduction of Irish Art Metal Work*, 1893

National Museum of Antiquities of Scotland, *Brooches in Scotland*, 1966

Waterhouse & Co, *Antique Irish Brooches*, 1872

6 CERAMICS

Bedford, J. *Talking about Teapots*, 1964

Bristowe, W.S. *Victorian China Fairings*, 2nd 1971

Clarke, H.G. *The Pictorial Pot Lid Book*, 1960

Emery, N. 'William Henry Goss and Goss Heraldic China', *Journal of Ceramic History 4*, 1971

Hillier, Bevis 'Souvenirs in Porcelain', *The Times,* 12. vi. 1971

Jewitt, L. *The Ceramic Art of Great Britain*, 2nd ed 1877

Kiddell, A.J.B. Account of the life of William Absolon, the Yarmouth decorator of ceramics and glass, *English Ceramic Circle Transactions*, 5, i (1960)

Moore, N.H. *The Old China Book,* 1903, reprinted 1935 (lists manufacturers of topographical views in blue and white)

7 METAL SOUVENIRS

Brown, R.A. *Horse Brasses and their Origin*, 1951

8 BUT IT IS A SOUVENIR

Klamkin, M. *The Collector's Book of Boxes,* 1970 and 1972

Haynes, E.B. *Glass through the Ages*, 1948

Morris, B. *Victorian Embroidery*, 1962

154

Acknowledgements

I would like to express my gratitude to all those who answered letters and questions and, in particular, the staffs of the following:

Libraries: Dublin, Galway, the Manx Museum, Scarborough, Southend-on-Sea, Weston-super-Mare, Whitby.

Museums: City of Birmingham, City of Norwich, Dresden, National Museum of Antiquities of Scotland, Edinburgh, Stoke-on-Trent, Ulster Folk Museum, Umalecko-przmyslové, Prague, Victoria and Albert (Bethnal Green) Museum, Wolverhampton.

Organisations: British Ceramic Manufacturers' Federation, Bord Failte (Irish Tourist Board), CoSIRA, the Highlands and Islands Development Board.

I particularly appreciated help from individuals, including Mr D.G. Bennett, Miss N.H. Copping, Dr Eric Glasgow, Mr J. Graham-Campbell, Miss G. Grill, Mr D.B. Hague, Mr H.G. Morgan, Mrs E.M. Morgan, Mr D.H. Musselwhite and Mr Ian Purkis; and firms such as Wm Briggs & Co Ltd, Devon Leathercrafts Ltd, Heathergems Ltd, Charles Iles & Gomm Ltd, Pearson Page Jewsbury Co Ltd and Shell International Petroleum Co Ltd.

I am indebted to Mrs M. Bridson, Mr G.W. Chaplin, Mr F. Cowin, Miss M. Devereau, Mr M. Faragher, Mrs D. Fielding, Mr A. Gather and Mr D. Hume for the loan of souvenirs as illustrations. I would also like to acknowledge the skill and patience of the following people and organisations who supplied the photographs: A. Gather for plate 18; Board Failté, 3 and 5; City of Birmingham museum, 6, 9 and 15; Council for Small Industries in Rural Areas, 8, 9 and 24; Devon Leathercrafts, 25; Highlands and Islands Development Board, 4; Keig's Ltd, 1, 14, 21, 22 and 27; Manx Museum, 19 and 20; Manx Press, 2, 10, 11, 12, 13 and 16; Pearson Page and Jewsbury Co Ltd, 22 and 23; P. Thornton Mallaby, 28; Shell Photographic Service, 29.

Index

s = souvenirs Individual resorts are listed under their own name only when something constructive is said about their amenities, development etc. A list of resorts from which localised souvenirs are cited or illustrated appears under *Resorts*. Similarly Birmingham and Newcastle-upon-Tyne have entries as places of manufacture but their souvenirs are under *Resorts*. *Pl 1/73* indicates illustration. Since these are not otherwise listed, plates are cited by number and page number, line drawings by page alone.

Advertising of s (including directory entries), 18–19, 25, 26–7, 29–31, 35, 49, 69, 74, 76, 82, 103, 104, 112–3, 124–6, 129

Agents for, ceramic s manufacturers, 96, 103; crested ceramics, 86, 90 *pl 17/88*

America, British-made s for, 33; German-made s for, 119; tourists from, 20 – *See also* USA

'a present from . . .', 16, 36, 60, 94, 107, 114

Arran, Isle of, use of ferns from, 35

Art Deco, in s designs, 77

Art Nouveau in s designs, 75, 77, 81, *pl 14/68*

Athens, Classical s from, 9

'a trifle from . . .', 16, 36

Australia, s for, 33

Austria, s manufacturers, 93, 99 (mainly ceramics qv)

Barbados, 'a present from . . .', 56

basketry and rushwork, 41–3, *43, pl 5/ 26, 26/120*

'Bilston' enamel, 16

Birmingham, s manufacturers in, 33, 67, 77, 79, 109, 111, 114

Blackpool: 133; catchment area of, 14; development of, 15; seaside rock made in, 23; visitor numbers, 22

bloaters (Yarmouth) as s, 16

Bohemia, glass s from, 122, *pl 26/120* – *see also* ceramics

Bournmouth 14, 131

boxes, ceramic, 96; enamel, 16; metal, 114–115; snuff, 28–30, 114, 117; wooden, 28–37 – *see also* needlework accessories

Brighton, 14, 36, 132; visitor numbers 22

Bristowe, W. S. (*Victorian China fairings*), 95, 154

Burns, Robert – *see* Scotland; Burnsiana

Celluloid 116–7

Celtic designs in s, 7, 72, 74–5, 80–82, *pl 14/68, 72*

Ceramics ancient, 9; Austrian-made, 93, 99; Belleek, 91–3, 97, *pl 16/85*; boxes, 96, 144–5; craft 94–5, *pl 1/13 21/106*; crested wares, 89–93, 98 *pl 17/88,* appendix 5; Doulton, 105; German-made, 7, 91, 93–4, 95, 96, 98, 99, 107, 108, *pl 16/85, 20/96* and *appendices 5 and 6*; Goss, 17, 84, 86–9, *pl 17/88, 18/90* and *appendix 6* lithophanes, 97–8; Parian, 93, 98–9; pink ware, 102–3, *pl 1/13, 18/90* and appendix 6, 150–1; plaques, 98–9, *appendix 6* p 148–9; ribbon plates, 99–100, 149, *pl 1/13*; Staffordshire, 89–90, 97, 103–5, 107, *pl 20/96*; Sunderland, 17, 100–102; Thuringian-made, 97, *pl 20/96*; transfer-printed, 103–5, *pl 16/85*

Cheddar, cheese, 16; gorge, 11
China, s made in (including Hong Kong and Taiwan), 42, 78, 100, *pl 10/52, 11/53*
Chlorociboria aeruginascens, 37
collage, 45–8, 112
Cornwall, visitor figures, 22
CoSIRA, 22, 41, 95; acknowledgement, 155
corkwork, 44–5
craft potteries – *see* Ceramics
craft s, 5, 39–41, *pl 3, 4*
cream, Cornish, Devonshire, as s, 16
Crete, ancient s in/from 9, 10, 50; Goss model of Minoan pot, 86
Czechoslovakia, ceramic s made in, 91, 93, 99–100

edible s, 16
'Elsinore' bowls, 108
embedding in 'plastic' resin, 57–8, 112, *pl 11/53, 26/120*
emblems of localities, Cornish chough, *pl 26/120*; Irish harp, 28, 72, 93, *pl 15/73*; Killarney fern, 28, *27*; Lincoln imp, 17, 70, 109, *pl 22/110*; Manx cat, 17, 76, 109, 129; Scottish heather, 70; Shakespeare's bust, 17, 70, 109; shamrock, 14, 17, 28, 70, 72, 76, 93, *pl 15/73* three-legs (IOM), 17, 70, 97, 111, 112, 113, 114, 127, 129, *pl 1/13, 14/68/15/*

73, *28/123*, 27, 79
embroidery designs, 127–8; packs, 128, *pl 2/18*
Egypt s of/from, 10
Erasmus, on s worn by pilgrims, 10

Fairings, 93, 98
fern ware, 35, 49
Festival of Britain, 1951, 57
figures – *see* ceramics
fossils as s – *see* geology
France, British-made s for, 33, 87
Frinton, 14, 132

Geology; Ailsa Craig stone, 15–16, 59, 66; Alum Bay sand, 44, 59–61; Charnwood stone, 66; Connemara marble, 61–2, 72, 74, *pl 5/26, 14/68*; Cornish marble 65–6, *pl 13/64*; Derbyshire, 59, 62–5, *pl 12/61, 13/64*; fossils 59; Iona marble, 15–16, 19, 81, *pl 14/68*; jewellery, 67–70 *pl 14/68*; Portsoy marble, 2', 66, *pl 12/61*; resorts noted for, 59 and *appendix 4*, 140–1; Whitby jet, 28, 67–9
Gemma, trade mark, 34, 39, 93, 96, 107, 113 – *see* Czechoslovakia
German-made s 33 *see also* ceramics, glass, medalets
Glasgow, Dr Eric, research by, 19
Glass; engraved, 122; figures, 122; friggers 24, 122; paperweights, 119–121, *pl 1/13*; pressed, 122–4, *pl 28/123*; silver, 124
good luck symbols, 76–8, 95
Great Exhibition of 1851, 7, 25, 34–5, 38, 60, 61, 65, 71, 74, 75, 76, 81, 125, 127, 128, 72
Greece, s of/in ancient, 9, 10 – *see also* Crete

Handkerchiefs, 128–9
Highlands and Islands Development Board, 95; acknowledgements, 155

holidays, development of modern pattern, 12–14
Holy Land, s of, 9, 22
horn; beakers, 47; craft, 46–7, *pl 9*; Irish s (hoof), 46 jewellery 82, *pl 14/68*

Ireland; arbutus, 25–6; bog oak, 26–8, *pl 2/18*; Celtic design, revived 7, 72–4, *72*; Claddagh ring, 75, 76, 82; Connemara marble, 61–2, 72, 74, *pl 5/26, 14/68*; craft s, *pl 5/26*; development of s. trade 14; 'diamonds', 27, 70; freshwater pearls, 71; jewellery, 72–5, *pl 14/68, 15/73, 74*; rushwork, 42–3 *pl 5/26, 26/120*; St Brigid's cross, 42–3, *43*; shillelagh 28
Irish Tourist Board (Bord Failté), research into s market, 20–21; s promotion, 22
Isle of Man; Douglas, 15; *national* newspapers, 19; peculiar s, 61; perfumes, 19, 124–7; s made in, 111, 113, 129; s trade in, 19–20; textiles, 127–9
Isle of Wight, unique s, 44, 59–61; 'diamonds', 70

Japanese-made s, 33, 44, 78, 94, 95, 100, 117
joke s, 17, 116
Kerr, Hugh, modern wooden jewelery by, 40
kippers, Manx, 16

Laxey silver, 112–3, *pl 27/121*
lead figures, 113
leatherwork, craft, *pl 24/117*; crested 118–9, *pl 23/118*

metal-plated natural objects, 78–9, *pl 14/68*
Margate, 14, 15, 132
matchboxes, 94, 114
medalets, 113
minerals as s, 16

Minoan – *see* Crete
Mont St Michel, s associated with pilgrimage to, 12, 51
Museums; Ashmolean, Oxford, 86; Bethnal Green (branch of V & A), 53, 54 Birmingham, *32, 37,* 38, *73,* 74; Geological (South Ken), 62, 64; Guille Alles (St Peter Port), 55; Manx, 48, 56, 70, 77, 127, 141; Weston-Super-Mare, 121, 141

needlework, designs for, 127–8; s packs, 128, *pl 1/13, 2/18*; tools/accessories 7, 25, 28, 32–6, 54, 109, 138–9; *pl 1/1˞ 2/18, 6/32, 7/37, pl 26/120*
Norris, K. & P., modern wooden jewellery, 40

peasant ('ethnic') items as s 22, 39, 42
pearls, freshwater, 28, 70–71; marine mussel, 7; shell, bag; brooches etc, 77–8; charms, 78; *pl 10/22*
peepshow views, 116–7, *pl 2/18*
pens, 117, 136
pilgrims' badges, 10, 51, *11*
Pinto, E. H. & E. R., research into woodwares, 31, 35
pixies, lucky, 66, 95
Pompeii s shells in, 51
Portugal, cork s made in, 44
potichomania, 60
pottery – *see* Ceramics
Pratt pot lids, 9, 16
Prices of souvenirs, 19–20, 127

Queen Victoria, influence of, 32, 67, 80; Jubilee, 60, 123–4; patronage, 28, 72, 74, 75; seaweed album, 47

Railways, effect of growth on holiday trade, 12–15, 25
Ramsgate, 15
registration of designs, 125; key to number 135

Resorts/districts, cited s from; *entries for islands, Scilly, Wight etc, under their names, not individual resorts.*

Aberystwyth, 47
Aberdeen, 144; Abergavenny, 144; Aberystwyth, 47; Barmouth, *pl 17/88*; Barnstaple, *pl 21/106*; Belfast, 114; Blackpool, 14, 17, 41, *pl 1/13, 17/88*; Bournmouth, *pl 16/85, 17/88*; Brighton, 36, 117, 146, 147, 148, 150, *pl 2/18*; Conway, 71; Cornwall, 65–6, 69, *pl 1/13, 12/61, 13/64, 21/106, 26/120*; Derbyshire, 19, 62–5, *pl 12/61, 13/64, 14/68*; Durham, 151; Ely, 147; Glastonbury, *pl 21/106*; Holyhead, 148 Hull, *pl 1 and 16/85*; Ireland, 25–8 42–3, 61–2, 71, 72–5, 91–3, 94; *pl 4/21, 5/26, 15/73*; Claddagh ring, 74 – 5; Connemara marble, 61–2, *pl 14/68*; Killarney, 25, 46; Larne, 114; Isle of Man, 48–50, 96–8, 113, 114, 144, *pl 1/13, 10/52, 11/53, 14/68, 16/85, 17/88, 20/96, 26/120; 27, 79*; Castletown, 105, 144, 149, *as last*; Douglas, 7, 97, 101, 144–50, *as first*; Glen Helen, 148; Kirk Braddan, 45, 148, *pl 12/61*; Port Erin, 145, 147, 148, *pl 27/121*; Peel, 146, *pl 18/90*; Port St Mary, *pl 17/88*; Ramsey, 147, *pl 16/85*; Isle of Wight, 70, Alum Bay, 59–61; Osborne House/cork, 44; Isles of Scilly, 90, *pl 17/88*; Jersey, 70; Kenilworth, 103; Liverpool, 128, 144, 147; London, 26, 103, 122, *pl 2/18, 16/85, 26/120*; Lowestoft, 148; Llandudno, 146, 147; Llangollen, 145; Lyme Regis, 59, *pl 14/68*; Kendal (Abbey Horn Works), *pl 9/46*; Margate, 7, 36; Newcastle-upon-Tyne, *pl 16/85*; Portobello, *pl 16/85*; Portsmouth, *pl 17/88*; Pwllheli, 41; Rhyl, *pl 17/88*; Rye, 105; Salisbury *pl 17/88*; Scarborough, *pl 18/88*; Shetland 78, *pl 1/13*; Snowdon, 54–5; Somerset, 41, *pl 1/13, 21/106*; South-port 150; St Ives, *pl 21/106*; Stow-on-the-Wold, *pl 21/106*; Stratford-on-Avon, 2–5, 79, 99, 148, 149, *pl 2/18*; Sunderland, 100–101; Symons Yat, 144; Tunbridge Wells – *see under* woodware; Walmer, 148; Warwickshire, *pl 17/88*; Weston-Super-Mare, 121, 147, *pl 1/13*; Weymouth, 147; Whitby, 67, 69, 103; Whitehaven, *pl 17/88*; Winchester, *pl 17/88*; Windsor, 111; Yarmouth, 122, 148

rock, seaside, 20, 23
Sadler & Green, L'pool, 32, 104
St Brigid's crosses, 42–3, *43*
St James of Composteila (scallop s), 10–12, 51
St Michael's Mount, 69
sailors' gifts (shells), 56
scent, 1, 124–6, *pl 1/13*
Scirpus lacustris
Scotland: Ailsa Craig stone, 15–16, 59, 66; Burnssiana etc 8, 35, 128; craft pottery, *pl 21/106*; deerhide s, *pl 24/117*; freshwater pearls, 70–71; jewellery, 7, 40, 80–3, embroidery packs, 128, *pl 14/68*; luckenbooth brooches, 82–3, *82*; marble: 66, Iona, 15–16, 19, 81, Portsoy, 22, *pl 12/61*; plastic embedding, *pl 26/120*; s shops, *pl 4/21*; s trade development, 15–16, 22, 134; woodware 28–36, pl 6/32
seaweed s, 47–50
Shell, 53
shells in ancient times as s, 50–51; medieval s, 11–12; shellwork, 51–8 *pl 10/51, 11/52*
Sidmouth, 69, 131
Simla, s of, 120
Southend-on-Sea, 14–15, 132
Southport, 19, 133
Spa (Belgium), products of as s, 24, 29, 39
Sparta, (Laconia), stone from as s, 10
sticks, walking, 28, 40
Stratford-on-Avon, 17, 18

tartan, in s trade, 34; use outside Scotland at early date, 34
tawdry/St Audrey's fair, 12
topigraphical views, sources of 17, 103, 104–5 – *see also* ceramics, woodware
Tunbridge Wells, 24

USA, source of supply for craft s makers, 57, 66

Visitors, origins of, 14, 20

Wakes weeks, 13
Wales: dragon, *pl 26/120*; early resorts in, 14; figures, 145 Wales love spoons,

pl 8/38 modern resorts, 31, 131, 132
Walton-on-the-Naze, 15
water transport, importance of, 15, 36
Weston-super-Mare, 15, 131
wishing wells, 11
Woodware: arbutus, 25–8; bog oak, 26–8, *27*, *pl 1/13*, *2/18*; foreign, 38–9; modern, 39, *pl 5/26*, *8/38*; Scottish, 28–36 – Laurencekirk, 29–30, Mauchline, 7, 30–33, *pl 2/18*, *6/32*, *12/61*; Tunbridge ware, 16, 36–8, *pl 7/37*, (*pl 26/120* T-type)
Worthing, 14, 133
Writing accessories, 18, 26, 27–8, 32, 44, 136